GIGANTIC CINEMA

BY ALICE OSWALD

POETRY
The Thing in the Gap-Stone Stile
Dart
Woods etc.
A Sleepwalk on the Severn
Weeds and Wild Flowers
Memorial
Falling Awake
Nobody

EDITOR
The Thunder Mutters: 101 Poems for the Planet
Thomas Wyatt: Selected Poems

BY PAUL KEEGAN

EDITOR
The Penguin Book of English Verse
Collected Poems of Ted Hughes

GIGANTIC CINEMA

A WEATHER ANTHOLOGY

edited by
Alice Oswald & Paul Keegan

W. W. NORTON & COMPANY
Independent Publishers Since 1923

For information about special discounts for bulk purchases,
please contact W. W. Norton Special Sales at
specialsales@wwnorton.com or 800-233-4830

Manufacturing by Lakeside Book Company

Library of Congress Cataloging-in-Publication Data

Names: Oswald, Alice, 1966– editor. | Keegan, Paul, editor.
Title: Gigantic cinema : a weather anthology /
edited by Alice Oswald & Paul Keegan.
Description: First American edition. | New York :
W. W. Norton & Company, 2021. | Includes index.
Identifiers: LCCN 2021012936 |
ISBN 9780393540758 (paperback) |
ISBN 9780393540765 (epub)
Subjects: LCSH: Nature–Literary collections. |
Weather–Literary collections. | Weather in literature. |
Meteorology in literature.
Classification: LCC PN6071.N3 W47 2021 | DDC 808.8/036–dc23
LC record available at https://lccn.loc.gov/2021012936

W. W. Norton & Company, Inc.
500 Fifth Avenue, New York, N.Y. 10110
www.wwnorton.com

W. W. Norton & Company Ltd.
15 Carlisle Street, London W1D 3BS

1 2 3 4 5 6 7 8 9 0

for Kevin Mount

CONTENTS

PREFACE

' ... a sunny, misty, cloudy, dazzling, howling, omniform, Day.'

Weather has no plot. It is all mutability and vicissitude, and so is this anthology. It is structured as a notional 'omniform' day, containing all weathers – and its three hundred entries, which range from the literary to the scientific, to jottings, journals, letters and many more, in their various voices prompting and curtailing each other, are a loud part of that day's noise. What we are offering is an impression of weather as non-stop interruption, although even that impression will be interrupted by others in the pages that follow.

In his essay on 'My First Acquaintance with Poets', William Hazlitt describes a walking holiday along the Bristol Channel with his new friend: 'A thunder-storm came on while we were at the inn, and Coleridge was running out bare-headed to enjoy the commotion of the elements ... '. 'Bareheadedness' has been another of the aspirations of this anthology. Our texts are hatless. Authors and titles have been pushed aside (to the foot of the page or the back of the book) so that extracts may be exposed to each other – one excerpt summoning up the weather of the next – with no distinction between prose and poetry, or between poems with authors and without authors, or between fiction and report. There are almost no dates on the page, since weather occupies what Wallace Stevens called 'the area between is and was'. We'd like you to read this book with no hat, no coat, no preconceptions, encountering each voice abruptly, as an exclamation brought on by the weather.

Coleridge, who described positioning his mirror so that he could see the changing cloud-light while shaving, maintained a bareheaded attention throughout his notebooks. Among daily weather memos ('the sky is covered with whitish and with dingy cloudage, thin dingiest Scud close under the moon and one side of it moving, all else moveless'), he recorded his wish to write 'a set of playbills for the Vale of Keswick – for every day in the year – announcing each day the performance, by his Supreme Majesty's Servants, Clouds, Waters, Sun, Moon, Stars, &c.' *Gigantic Cinema* is that kind of performance – and this way of speaking has something to do with the weather's play-like control of our attention, on the stage of the day. 'Enter a cloud' says W.S. Graham, and this phrase could be the title of any of our entries, like one of Shakespeare's stage directions ('Enter mariners, wet'), or like Elizabeth Bishop's fantasia of weather as stage machinery: 'Now the storm goes away again in a series / of small, badly lit battle-scenes, / each in "Another part of the field".' Virginia Woolf, ill in bed and staring at the sky, had the same sensation of being someone in the weather's audience, and her delirious description provides the voice-over for this anthology: 'this incessant making up of shapes and casting them down, this buffeting of clouds together, and drawing vast trains of ships and wagons from North to South, this incessant ringing up and down of curtains of light and shade, this interminable experiment with gold shafts and blue shadows, with veiling the sun and unveiling it, with making rock ramparts and wafting them away… One should not let this gigantic cinema play perpetually to an empty house.'

Any attempt to communicate all that buffeting is bound to be, as she says, both interminable and experimental. After all, what is not weather? Medieval writers thought honey was a form of weather; Homer described speech as a kind of snow; a report in the *Atlantic Monthly* in 1916 suggested that the 'tremendous expenditure of ammunition' on the Western Front had itself become a meteorological force; Audubon witnessed an eclipse of the sun by passenger pigeons. If you restrict weather to the air, then you miss out on Maeterlink's phototropic flowers or Mandelstam's pebble, or the stone tortoises of Victor Segalen. If you relate it to light, then you forget the blindness of John Hull, stuck at the musical centre of a rainstorm. It is tempting to call anything weather when it is beyond human control, but that fails to account for the rain-invocations in Fraser's *Golden Bough* or conversations with the sun in Daniel Paul Schreber's record of his illness, or Pueblo Indian rituals of magical weather-thinking. Distracted by all these examples, we have widened and widened our definition. In the end, working with the hunch that weather might be nothing smaller than undated Time, we have included dreams, ghosts, birds, volcanos, nuclear explosions, moods, echoes, souls, luck, smoke... and a good deal more.

Before it became a science of constant weather, meteorology (meaning the art of looking up) was the study of individual meteors: manifestations of the unusual, of rogue individuals in nature. Defoe could still report – of the Great Storm of 1703 – that 'the air was full of Meteors and fiery Vapours'. We include a lot of extraordinary weather, to get some purchase on what ancestors thought was really happening in the sky; but we have also tried to listen to the quieter, closer weathers that appear in diaries, journals, notebooks, letters – writings which report with immediacy on unstable phenomena and are themselves unstable, unanchored in the literary: places where the everyday, in the form of weather, progressively stole into literature.

But the story of how weather enters writing, at first as spectacle, then as a constant marginal presence, goes beyond the scale of any anthology. Over a period of five years, we have been gathering examples, most of which have not been included, and it's important that a reader should construe this whole endeavour as absurd, fragmentary, unfinishable. There is a great storm of writings pushing at the edges of the book. Perhaps the only way to convey this uncontainable excess is to quote from one of them – Curzio Malaparte's account of his time as a war correspondent, covering the Eastern Front in 1941:

> On the third day a huge fire flared in the Raikkola forest. Men, horses and trees clutched within the circle of fire sent out awful cries. The rangers, firing through that wall of smoke and flames, blocked every avenue of escape. Mad with terror, the horses of the Soviet artillery – there were almost a thousand of them – hurled themselves into the furnace and broke through the besieging flames and machine guns. Many perished within the flames, but most of them succeeded in reaching the shores of Lake Ladoga and threw themselves into the water.
>
> The lake is not deep there, not more than six feet; but a hundred yards from the shore the bottom suddenly drops. Pressed within the narrow space (the lakeshore curves inward

a this point, forming a small bay) between the deeper water and the barrier of fire, the horses clustered, shuddering with cold and fear, their heads stretched out above the surface. Those nearer to land were scorched by the flames and reared and struggled to hoist themselves onto the backs of the others, trying to push a way through by biting and kicking. And while they were still madly struggling, the ice gripped them.

The north wind swooped down during the night. (The north wind blows from the Murmansk Sea, like an angel of doom, crying aloud, and the land suddenly dies.) The cold became frightful. Suddenly, with the peculiar vibrating noise of breaking glass, the water froze. The heat balance was broken, and the sea, the lakes, the rivers froze. In such instances, even sea waves are gripped in mid-air and become rounded ice waves suspended in the void.

On the following day, when the first ranger patrols, their hair singed, their faces blackened by smoke, cautiously stepped over the warm ashes in the charred forest and reached the lakeshore, a horrible and amazing sight met their eyes. The lake looked like a vast sheet of white marble on which rested hundreds upon hundreds of horses' heads. They appeared to have been chopped off cleanly with an ax. Only the heads stuck out of the crust of ice. And they were all facing the shore. The white flames of terror still burnt in their wide-open eyes. Closer to the shore a tangle of wildly rearing horses rose from the prison of ice ….

There is no let up. That passage drifted in among several others when the book was already at the printers. A metre-high heap of other samples had already been rejected as too indoor or too convoluted. Our ruling idea was to have no ideas: to dispense with writing 'about' weather, writing that knows what it's talking about. Instead we have preferred writing that is 'like' weather, that has the sovereignty of sheer event. As if the weather were to write itself (as it does in Apollinaire's calligramme of rain). So that even the most discursive of the texts included have a way of speaking – telegraphic, visceral – that 'buffets' us, indicating an outdoor world moving behind the language.

So, events rather than thoughts. But these definitions are not exact. Wherever you draw a line, as with Paul Muldoon's 'Boundary Commission', there is weather on both sides. (like the fog in the drawing-room, in Nathaniel Hawthorne's London notebooks). Weather interrupts thinking and shares inconsequence with it, as Thoreau recognised when he dreamt of compiling 'a meteorological journal of the mind'. You can no more prevent thought than you can prevent rain, and the words we think in are part of this squallishness. For Dr. Johnson, 'words are hourly shifting their relations, and can no more be ascertained in a dictionary, than a grove, in the agitation of a storm, can be accurately delineated from its picture in the water.' Weather as a name for the shock and luck of encountering language or reacting to the elements, weather as an affliction of thought or a gift of idea, weather as impossible excess or interruption or distraction or simple outsidedness – all these visions of a force beyond our control are wonderfully liberating, And we want the anthology to capture these irresponsibilities.

To concentrate on something as erratic as the weather has an immediate and disturbing effect on the imagination. This anthology will not add to the image of Nature as a suffering solid. Instead it attends to patterns and forces, things that are invisible, ephemeral, sudden, catastrophic, seasonal and endless: air's manifold appearances. Gilbert White took it for granted that 'the weather of a district is undoubtedly part of its natural history'. The anthology takes seriously such a thought, and its scale is small. It privileges the perceivable, the particular, the local over the global, the 'now' of raindrops. Even so, this weather constantly frames the human figure as tiny, besieged, exposed. Not only can we never leave the performance, but often it turns on us, like God goading his audience from inside the whirlwind: 'Where wast thou when I laid the foundations of the earth? Who hath laid the measures thereof, if thou knowest?' The height of the weather is a measure of man. This anthology has tried to get the proportions right. If the Anthropocene is us, and is upon us, we are being orphaned by it on a scale that has no measure. One way of saying this is that weather is what we stand to lose.

1.

The owl was requested
To do as much as he knew how.
He only hooted and told of the morning star.
And hooted again and told of the dawn.

2.

The Sun woke me this morning loud
and clear, saying 'Hey! I've been
trying to wake you up for fifteen
minutes. Don't be so rude, you are
only the second poet I've ever chosen
to speak to personally

       so why
aren't you more attentive? If I could
burn you through the window I would
to wake you up. I can't hang around
here all day.'

     'Sorry, Sun, I stayed
up late last night talking to Hal.'

'When I woke up Mayakovsky he was
a lot more prompt' the Sun said
petulantly. 'Most people are up
already waiting to see if I'm going
to put in an appearance.'

       I tried
to apologize 'I missed you yesterday.'
'That's better' he said. 'I didn't
know you'd come out.' 'You may be
wondering why I've come so close?'
'Yes' I said beginning to feel hot
wondering if maybe he wasn't burning me
anyway.

    'Frankly I wanted to tell you
I like your poetry. I see a lot

on my rounds and you're okay. You may
not be the greatest thing on earth, but
you're different. Now, I've heard some
say you're crazy, they being excessively
calm themselves to my mind, and other
crazy poets think that you're a boring
reactionary. Not me.
                          Just keep on
like I do and pay no attention. You'll
find that people always will complain
about the atmosphere, either too hot
or too cold too bright or too dark, days
too short or too long.
                          If you don't appear
at all one day they think you're lazy
or dead. Just keep right on, I like it.

And don't worry about your lineage
poetic or natural. The Sun shines on
the jungle, you know, on the tundra
the sea, the ghetto. Wherever you were
I knew it and saw you moving. I was waiting
for you to get to work.

                          And now that you
are making your own days, so to speak,
even if no one reads you but me
you won't be depressed. Not
everyone can look up, even at me. It
hurts their eyes.'
                          'Oh Sun, I'm so grateful to you!'

'Thanks and remember I'm watching. It's
easier for me to speak to you out
here. I don't have to slide down
between buildings to get your ear.
I know you love Manhattan, but
you ought to look up more often.

                                And
always embrace things, people earth
sky stars, as I do, freely and with
the appropriate sense of space. That
is your inclination, known in the heavens
and you should follow it to hell, if
necessary, which I doubt.
                                Maybe we'll
speak again in Africa, of which I too
am specially fond. Go back to sleep now
Frank, and I may leave a tiny poem
in that brain of yours as my farewell.'

'Sun, don't go!' I was awake
at last. 'No, go I must, they're calling
me.'
        'Who are they?'
                                Rising he said 'Some
day you'll know. They're calling to you
too.' Darkly he rose, and then I slept.

3.

I have often thought of writing a set of *Play-bills* for the vale of
Keswick – for every day in the Year – announcing each Day the
Performances by his Supreme Majesty's Servants, Clouds, Waters,
Sun, Moon, Stars, &c.

4.

But as for the faces of the Sky they are so many, that many of them
want proper names, & therefore it will be convenient to agree upon
some determinate ones, by which the most usuall may be in brief
exprest.

As let *Cleer Blew* signify a very cleer sky without any cloudes or
Exhalations.

Checkerd blew, a cleer Sky with many great white round clouds, such as are very usuall in Summer.

Hazy, a Sky that looks whitish by reason of the thickness of the higher parts of the air, by some Exhalations not form'd into Cloudes.

Thick, a Sky more whiten'd by a greater company of Vapours. These do usually make the *Luminaries* looke bearded or hairy & are oftentimes the cause of the appearance of Rings & Haloes about the Sun as well as the Moon.

Overcast, when the Vapours so whiten and thicken the air, that the Sun cannot break through. And of this there are very many degrees which may be exprest by *a little, much, more, very much* overcast, &c.

Let *Hairy* signify a Sky that has many small thin & high Exhalations, which resemble locks of hair, or flakes of hemp or flax. Whose varieties may be exprest by *Straight* or *Curv*'d &c, according to the resemblance they bear.

Let *Water*'d signify a Sky that has many high thin & small clouds, looking almost like water'd Tabby, call'd in some places a Mackaril Sky from the Resemblance it has to the spots on the backs of those fishes.

Let a sky be calld *Waved* when those cloudes appear much bigger & lower, but much after the same manner.

Cloudy, when the Sky has many thick Dark cloudes.

Low'ring, when the sky is not only very much overcast, but hath also underneath many thick dark Clouds which threaten rain.

The Significations of *gloomy, foggy, misty, sleeting, driving, rainy, snowy,* reaches or racks *variable* &c are well known, they being very commonly used. There may be also severall faces of the Sky compounded of two or more of these, which may be intelligibly enough exprest by two or more of those names. It is likewise desirable, that the particulars may be entered (in the pages of a Booke in folio) in as few words as are sufficient to signifie them intelligibly and plainly.

5.

Ordinarily to look at the sky for any length of time is impossible.
Pedestrians would be impeded and disconcerted by a public sky-
gazer. What snatches we get of it are mutilated by chimneys and
churches, serve as a background for man, signify wet weather or fine,
daub windows gold, and, filling in the branches, complete the pathos
of dishevelled autumnal plane trees in London squares. Now, become
as the leaf or the daisy, lying recumbent, staring straight up, the sky is
discovered to be something so different from this that really it is a
little shocking. This then has been going on all the time without our
knowing it! – this incessant making up of shapes and casting them
down, this buffeting of clouds together, and drawing vast trains of
ships and waggons from North to South, this incessant ringing up
and down of curtains of light and shade, this interminable
experiment with gold shafts and blue shadows, with veiling the sun
and unveiling it, with making rock ramparts and wafting them away
– this endless activity, with the waste of Heaven knows how many
million horse power of energy, has been left to work its will year in
year out. The fact seems to call for comment and indeed for censure.
Some one should write to *The Times* about it. Use should be made of
it. One should not let this gigantic cinema play perpetually to an
empty house. But watch a little longer and another emotion drowns
the stirrings of civic ardour. Divinely beautiful it is also divinely
heartless. Immeasurable resources are used for some purpose which
has nothing to do with human pleasure or human profit. If we were
all laid prone, frozen, stiff, still the sky would be experimenting with
its blues and golds.

6.

Think of the storm roaming the sky uneasily
like a dog looking for a place to sleep in,
listen to it growling.

Think how they must look now, the mangrove keys
lying out there unresponsive to the lightning
in dark, coarse-fibred families,

where occasionally a heron may undo his head,
shake up his feathers, make an uncertain comment
when the surrounding water shines.

Think of the boulevard and the little palm trees
all stuck in rows, suddenly revealed
as fistfuls of limp fish-skeletons.

It is raining there. The boulevard
and its broken sidewalks with weeds in every crack
are relieved to be wet, the sea to be freshened.

Now the storm goes away again in a series
of small, badly lit battle-scenes,
each in 'Another part of the field'.

Think of someone sleeping in the bottom of a row-boat
tied to a mangrove root or the pile of a bridge;
think of him as uninjured, barely disturbed.

7.

The rain came abruptly at a time when no one expected it,
In the very heart of luminous days and glorious fruit crops.
        At daybreak
When the women opened the windows, everything
Was changed – leaden and damp. And everybody felt
As if someone had deceived them. However they were not
Enraged at all – only surly and speechless.

The soothing fragrance of the fields entered the houses
Like a broad pardon before they knew their error. Then
With the sacks they once used to carry grapes,
They made a coarsely cut effigy of the summer and filled it
With straw and scattered memories. For a moment
You thought they were going to burn it in the upper square

Like an ultimate splendour, like an inexplicable revenge. But no –
They left it there forsaken in the yellow solitude of September,
A straw statue, getting soaked, unprotesting, in the noiseless rain.

8.

21 September 1984. At five o'clock this morning I woke up to the sound
of rain. I went into my study and pressed my forehead against the
window pane. The house was completely still, and the streets outside
seemed to be deserted. I stood there motionless, hardly breathing,
concentrating everything on the sound of the rain.

First, I noticed the differences of place. Some sounds come from
the left of the window, some from the right, and I can trace these as
far as the corner of the house and around it. Now I pay attention to
the higher sounds, as the rain splatters on the wall above the window
and on the roof of the house itself. Below me the rain falls onto a
fence, the shrubbery and onto the ground itself.

Next, there are differences of speed. There is a slow, steady drip,
drip, drip, and a more rapid cascade, against the background of the
pitter-patter of the individual drops on the window pane. These vary
in speed as the rainstorm itself ebbs and flows, and some patterns of
sounds overtake others, a bit like the music of the American
minimalist composer Steve Reich.

I notice now that there are differences in intensity. Here a surface
is meeting the full force of the rain but here is a sheltered place. Over
there is a heavy splashing, not the sound of rain at all, but of collected
water overflowing from a blocked pipe or something like that.

Differences of pitch emerge. There is the high-pitched drumming
staccato as the drops fall on metal, the deeper duller impact on brick
or concrete, and I notice that the note being struck differs slightly
even from one window pane to another. There are differences in the
speed with which the water is travelling: it swishes, gurgles, pelts
along in a fury, comes and goes. There are differences in the volume.
On the window pane it is very loud. The panes of glass vibrate on my
forehead. The sounds diminish, layer upon layer, receding into the
faint distance as the rain falls on nearby trees. I wonder how far away

I can hear it falling. Can I make it out on the houses over the road? I can certainly hear it on the house next door.

This built up into a complex pattern. The more intensely I listened, the more I found I could discriminate, building block upon block of sound, noticing regularities and irregularities, filling dimension upon dimension. Complete silence was necessary. Even the slight sound of my breathing was enough to obscure some of the faintest details. It reminded me of the noise of the London Underground, which was similarly patterned into many textures, layers and shapes, so many positions and levels.

Is it true that the blind live in their bodies rather than in the world? I am aware of my body, just as I am aware of the rain. My body is similarly made up of many patterns, many different regularities and irregularities, extended in space from down there to up here. These dimensions and details reveal themselves more and more as I concentrate my attention upon them. Nothing corresponds visually to this realization. Instead of having an image of my body, as being in what we call the 'human form', I apprehend it now as these arrangements of sensitivities, a conscious space comparable to the patterns of the falling rain. The patterns of water envelop me in myriads of spots of awareness, and my own body is presented to me in the same way. There is a central area, of which I am barely conscious, and which seems to come and go. At the extremities, sensations fade into unconsciousness. My body and the rain intermingle, and become one audio-tactile, three-dimensional universe, within which and throughout the whole of which lies my awareness. This is in sharp contrast to the single-track line of consecutive speech which makes up my thoughts. This line of thought expressed in speech is not extended in space at all, but comes towards me like carriages in a goods train, one after the other, coming out of the darkness, passing under the floodlight of knowledge, and receding into memory. That line of consecutive thoughts is situated within the three-dimensional reality of the patterns of consciousness made up by the rain and my body, a bit like the axis of a spinning top. It could be otherwise however. If the rain were to stop, and I remain motionless here, there would be silence. My awareness of the world would again shrink to the extremities of my skin. If I were paralysed from the neck down, the area would again be curtailed. How far could this process go? At what point do I become only a line of thought-speech, without an environment of sensation and perception? What happens to the tracks when there is no longer ground to support the line? What happens to the spinning-top when only the axis is left? Where do thoughts come from? Upon what do they depend? Into how many worlds am I inserted? What is blindness?

9.

A *Gyges* Ring they beare about them still,
To be, and not seen when and where they will.
They tread on clouds, and though they sometimes fall,
They fall like dew, but make no noise at all.
So silently they one to th'other come,
As colours steale into the Peare or Plum,
And Aire-like, leave no pression to be seen
Where'er they met, or parting place has been.

10.

When as the first beams of the sun break through, the river still lies sleeping, wrapped in dreams of mist, we no more see it than it sees itself. Here already at our feet is the river, but a little farther on the view is blocked, and we are aware only of nothingness, of a fog through which the eye cannot penetrate. To paint, at one spot on the canvas, not what one sees, because one can see nothing, nor what one does not see, because one ought never to paint what one has not seen, but *the fact of not seeing*, so that the failure of the eye which cannot pierce the mist, is imparted to the canvas as to the river, is beautiful indeed.

11.

THOR.　　Say, Dwarf, for it seems to me
　　　　　There is nothing you do not know: (…)

　　　　　What are clouds called, that carry rain,
　　　　　In all the worlds there are?

ALVIS.   *Clouds* by men, *Hope-of-Showers* by gods,
                 Wind-Ships by Vanes,
        By giants *Drizzle-Hope*, by elves *Weather-Might*,
                 In Hel *Helmet-of-Darkness*.

THOR.   What is wind called, that widely fares
        In all the worlds there are?

ALVIS.   *Wind* by men, *Woe-Father* by gods,
              By holy powers *The Neigher*,
        The Shouter by giants, *Travelling-Tumult* by elves,
              Squall-Blast they call it in Hel.

THOR.   What is calm called, that cannot stir,
        In all the worlds there are?

ALVIS.   *Calm* by men, *Stillness* by gods,
              Idle-Wind by vanes,
        Over-Warmth by giants, by elves *Day-Quiet*,
             And *Day-Rest* by dwarves (…)

THOR.   Never have I met such a master of lore
        With such a wealth of wisdom.
        I talked to trick you, and tricked you I have.
        Dawn has broken, Dwarf,
        Stiffen now to stone.

12.

Then a tremendous flash of light cut across the sky. Mr. Tanimoto has a distinct recollection that it travelled from east to west, from the city toward the hills. It seemed a sheet of sun. Both he and Mr. Matsuo reacted in terror – and both had time to react (for they were 3,500 yards, or two miles, from the center of the explosion). Mr. Matsuo dashed up the front steps into the house and dived among the bedrolls and buried himself there. Mr. Tanimoto took four or five steps and threw himself between two big rocks in the garden. He bellied up very hard against one of them. As his face was against the stone, he did not see what happened. He felt a sudden pressure, and then splinters and pieces of board and fragments of tile fell on him. He heard no roar. (Almost no one in Hiroshima recalls hearing any noise of the bomb. But a fisherman in his sampan on the Inland Sea near Tsuzu, the man with whom Mr. Tanimoto's mother-in-law and sister-in-law were living, saw the flash and heard a tremendous explosion; he was nearly twenty miles from Hiroshima, but the thunder was greater than when the B-29s hit Iwakuni, only five miles away).

When he dared, Mr. Tanimoto raised his head and saw that the rayon man's house had collapsed. He thought a bomb had fallen directly on it. Such clouds of dust had risen that there was a sort of twilight around. In panic, not thinking for the moment of Mr. Matsuo under the ruins, he dashed out into the street. He noticed as he ran that the concrete wall of the estate had fallen over – toward the house rather than away from it. In the street, the first thing he saw was a squad of soldiers who had been burrowing into the hillside opposite, making one of the thousands of dugouts in which the Japanese apparently intended to resist invasion, hill by hill, life for life; the soldiers were coming out of the hole, where they should have been safe, and blood was running from their heads, chests and backs. They were silent and dazed. Under what seemed to be a local dust cloud, the day grew darker and darker.

13.

My dear Tacitus,
You ask me to write you something about the death of my uncle so that the account you transmit to posterity is as reliable as possible. I am grateful to you, for I see that his death will be remembered forever if you treat it in your Histories. He perished in a devastation of the loveliest of lands, in a memorable disaster shared by peoples and cities, but this will be a kind of eternal life for him. He wrote a number of enduring works himself, but the imperishable nature of your writings will contribute greatly to his survival.

He was at Misenum in his capacity as commander of the fleet on the 24th of August [79 AD], when between 2 and 3 in the afternoon my mother drew his attention to a cloud of unusual size and appearance. He had had a sunbath, then a cold bath, and was reclining after dinner with his books. He called for his shoes and climbed up to where he could get the best view of the phenomenon. The cloud was rising from a mountain – at such a distance we couldn't tell which, but afterwards learned that it was Vesuvius. I can best describe its shape by likening it to a pine tree. It rose into the sky on a very long 'trunk' from which spread some 'branches'. I imagine it had been raised by a sudden blast, which then weakened, leaving the cloud unsupported so that its own weight caused it to spread sideways. Some of the cloud was white, in other parts there were dark patches of dirt and ash. The sight of it made the scientist in my uncle determine to see it from closer at hand.

He ordered a boat made ready. He offered me the opportunity of going along, but I preferred to study – he himself happened to have set me a writing exercise. As he was leaving the house he was brought a letter from Tascius' wife Rectina, who was terrified by the looming danger. Her villa lay at the foot of Vesuvius, and there was no way out except by boat. She begged him to get her away. He changed his plans. The expedition that started out as a quest for knowledge now called for courage. He launched the quadriremes and embarked himself, a source of aid for more people than just Rectina, for that delightful shore was a populous one. He hurried to a place from which others were fleeing, and held his course directly into danger. Was he afraid? It seems not, as he kept up a continuous observation of the various movements and shapes of that evil cloud, dictating what he saw.

Ash was falling onto the ships now, darker and denser the closer they went. Now it was bits of pumice, and rocks that were blackened and burned and shattered by the fire. Now the sea is shoal; debris from the mountain blocks the shore. He paused for a moment, wondering whether to turn back as the helmsman urged him. 'Fortune helps the brave,' he said. 'Head for Pomponianus.'

At Stabiae, on the other side of the bay formed by the gradually curving shore, Pomponianus had loaded up his ships even before the danger arrived, though it was visible and indeed extremely close, once it intensified. He planned to put out as soon as the contrary wind let up. That very wind carried my uncle right in, and he embraced the frightened man and gave him comfort and courage.

In order to lessen the other's fear by showing his own unconcern he asked to be taken to the baths. He bathed and dined, carefree or at least appearing so (which is equally impressive). Meanwhile, broad sheets of flame were lighting up many parts of Vesuvius; their light and brightness were the more vivid for the darkness of the night. To alleviate people's fears my uncle claimed that the flames came from the deserted homes of farmers who had left in a panic with the hearth fires still alight. Then he rested, and gave every indication of actually sleeping; people who passed by his door heard his snores, which were rather resonant since he was a heavy man. The ground outside his room rose so high with the mixture of ash and stones that if he had spent any more time there escape would have been impossible. He got up and came out, restoring himself to Pomponianus and the others who had been unable to sleep. They discussed what to do, whether to remain under cover or to try the open air. The buildings were being rocked by a series of strong tremors, and appeared to have come loose from their foundations and to be sliding this way and that. Outside, however, there was danger from the rocks that were coming down, light and fire-consumed as these bits of pumice were. Weighing the relative dangers they chose the outdoors; in my uncle's case it was a rational decision, others just chose the alternative that frightened them the least.

They tied pillows on top of their heads as protection against the shower of rock. It was daylight now elsewhere in the world, but here the darkness was darker and thicker than any night. They had torches and other lights, and decided to go down to the shore, to see from close up if anything was possible by sea. But it remained as rough and uncooperative as before. Resting in the shade of a sail he drank once or twice from the cold water he had asked for. Then came a smell of sulfur, announcing the flames, and the flames themselves, sending others into flight but reviving him. Supported by two small slaves he stood up, and immediately collapsed. As I understand it, his breathing was obstructed by the dust-laden air, and his innards, which were never strong and often blocked or upset, simply shut down. When daylight came again two days after he died, his body was found untouched, unharmed, in the clothing that he had had on. He looked more asleep than dead.

14.

*'and we should die of that roar which lies on the
other side of silence'* – George Eliot, *Middlemarch*

Dead dandelions, bald as drumsticks,
swaying by the roadside

like Hare Krishna pilgrims
bowing to the Juggernaut.

They have given up everything.
Gold gone and their silver gone,

humbled with dust, hollow,
their milky bodies tan

to the colour of annas.
The wind changes their identity:

slender Giacomettis, Doré's convicts,
Rodin's burghers of Calais

with five bowed heads
and the weight of serrated keys ...

They wither into mystery, waiting
to find out why they are,

patiently, before nirvana
when the rain comes down like vitriol.

15.

'It's going to rain tonight.'
'It's raining now,' I said.
'The radio said tonight.'
I drove him to school on his first day back after a sore throat and
fever. A woman in a yellow slicker held up traffic to let some children

cross. I pictured her in a soup commercial taking off her oilskin hat as she entered a cheerful kitchen where her husband stood over a pot of smoky lobster bisque, a smallish man with six weeks to live.

'Look at the windshield,' I said. 'Is that rain or isn't it?'

'I'm only telling you what they said.'

'Just because it's on the radio doesn't mean we have to suspend belief in the evidence of our senses.'

'Our senses? Our senses are wrong a lot more often than they're right. This has been proved in the laboratory. Don't you know about all those theorems that say nothing is what it seems? There's no past, present or future outside our own mind. The so-called laws of motion are a big hoax. Even sound can trick the mind. Just because you don't hear a sound doesn't mean it's not out there. Dogs can hear it. Other animals. And I'm sure there are sounds even dogs can't hear. But they exist in the air, in waves. Maybe they never stop. High, high, high-pitched. Coming from somewhere.'

'Is it raining, or isn't it?'

'I wouldn't want to have to say.'

'What if someone held a gun to your head?'

'Who, you?'

'Someone. A man in a trenchcoat and smoky glasses. He holds a gun to your head and says, "Is it raining or isn't it? All you have to do is tell the truth and I'll put away my gun and take the next flight out of here."'

'What truth does he want? Does he want the truth of someone travelling at almost the speed of light in another galaxy? Does he want the truth of someone in orbit around a neutron star? Maybe if these people could see us through a telescope we might look like we were two feet two inches tall and it might be raining yesterday instead of today.'

'He's holding a gun to *your* head. He wants your truth.'

'What good is my truth? My truth means nothing. What if this guy with the gun comes from a planet in a whole different solar system? What we call rain he calls soap. What we call apples he calls rain. So what am I supposed to tell him?'

'His name is Frank J. Smalley and he comes from St. Louis.'

'He wants to know if it's raining *now*, at this very minute?'

'Here and now. That's right.'

'Is there such a thing as now? "Now" comes and goes as soon as you say it. How can I say it's raining now if your so-called "now" becomes "then" as soon as I say it?'

'You said there was no past, present, or future.'

'Only in our verbs. That's the only place we find it.'

'Rain is a noun. Is there rain here, in this precise locality, at whatever time within the next two minutes that you choose to respond to the question?'

'If you want to talk about this precise locality while you're in a vehicle that's obviously moving, then I think that's the trouble with this discusssion.'

'Just give me an answer, okay, Heinrich?'

'The best I could do is make a guess.'

'Either it's raining or it isn't,' I said.

'Exactly. That's my whole point. You'd be guessing. Six of one, half dozen of the other.'

'But you *see* it's raining.'

'You see the sun moving across the sky. But is the sun moving across the sky or is the earth turning?'

'I don't accept the analogy.'

'You're so sure that's rain. How do you know it's not sulfuric acid from factories across the river? How do you know it's not fallout from a war in China? You want an answer here and now. Can you prove, here and now, that this stuff is rain? How do I know that what you call rain is really rain? What *is* rain anyway?'

'It's the stuff that falls from the sky and gets you what is called wet.'

'I'm not wet. Are you wet?'

'All right,' I said. 'Very good.'

'No, seriously, are you wet?'

'First-rate,' I told him. 'A victory for uncertainty, randomness and chaos.'

16.

Skywind, skillful disorder,
Strong tumult walking over there,
Wondrous man, rowdy-sounding,
World hero, with neither foot nor wing.

Yeast in cloud loaves, you were thrown out
Of sky's pantry, with not one foot,
How swiftly you run, and so well
This moment above the high hill.

Tell me, north wind of the cwm,
Your route, reliable hymn.
Over the lengths of the world you fly,
Tonight, hill weather, please stay high,
Ah man, go over Upper Aeron
Be lovely and cool, stay in clear tune.
Don't hang about or let that maniac,
Litigious Little Bow, hold you back,
He's poisonous. Society
And its goods are closed to me.

Thief of nests, though you winnow leaves
No one accuses you, nor impedes
You, no band of men, nor magistrate's hand,
Nor blue blade, nor flood, nor rain.
Indeed, no son of man can kill you,
Fire won't burn nor treason harm you.
You shall not drown, as you're aware,
You're never stuck, you're angle-less air.
No need of swift horse to get about,
Nor bridge over water, nor any boat.
No officer or force will hand you over
To court for fingering treetop feathers.
Sight cannot see you, wide-open den,
But thousands hear you, nest of great rain.

You are God's grace across the world,
The roar when breaking tops of oaks are hurled,
You hang clouds' notes in heaven's score
And dance athletically over moors
Dry-humoured, clever creature,
Over clouds' stepping-stones you travel far,
Archer on fields of snow up high,
Disperser of rubbish piles in loud cries.

Storm that's stirring up the sea
Randy surfer where land meets sea.
Bold poet, rhyming snowdrifts you are,
Sower, scatterer of leaves you are,
Clown of peaks, you get off scot-free,
Hurler of mad-masted, foaming sea.

I was lost once I felt desire
For Morfudd of the golden hair.
A girl has caused my disgrace,
Run up to her father's house,
Knock on the door, make him open
To my messenger before the dawn,
Find her if there's any way,
Give song to the voice of my sigh.
You come from unsullied stars,
Tell my noble, generous her:
For as long as I'm alive
I will be her loyal slave.
My face without her's a mess
If it's true she's not been faithless.

Go up high, see the one who's white,
Go down below, sky's favourite.
Go to Morfudd Llwyd the fair,
Come back safe, wealth of the air.

17.

The Wind – tapped like a tired Man –
And like a Host – 'Come in'
I boldly answered – entered then
My Residence within

A Rapid – footless Guest –
To offer whom a Chair
Were as impossible as hand
A Sofa to the Air –

No Bone had He to bind Him –
His Speech was like the Push
Of numerous Humming Birds at once
From a superior Bush –

His Countenance – a Billow –
His Fingers, as He passed
Let go a music – as of tunes
Blown tremulous in Glass –

He visited – still flitting –
Then like a timid Man
Again, He tapped – 'twas flurriedly –
And I became alone –

18.

– Tell me the substance from which Adam, the first man, was made.
– I tell you, from eight pounds' weight.
– Tell me, what are they called.
– I tell you, the first was a pound of earth, from which his flesh was
made. The second was a pound of fire; from which his blood came red
and hot. The third was a pound of wind; from which his breath was
given him. The fourth was a pound of cloud; whence his instability of
mind. The fifth was a pound of grace; whence his understanding and
thought. The sixth was a pound of blossoms; from which was given the
variety of his eyes. The seventh was a pound of dew; whence he got his
sweat. The eighth was a pound of salt; from which his tears were salt.

19.

       Their ground they stil made good,
And (in their silence and set powers) like fair still clouds they stood,
With which Jove crownes the tops of hills in any quiet day,
When Boreas and the ruder winds (that use to drive away
Aire's duskie vapors, being loose, in many a whistling gale)
Are pleasingly bound up and calme, and not a breath exhale:
So firmely stood the Greeks.

20.

    In 'P' sap, in 'Q' post,
in the fire-trench,
in Moggs Hole and Cats Post.
    An eastward alignment of troubled, ashen faces; delicate
mechanisms of nerve and sinew, grapple afresh, deal for another day;
ill-matched contesting, handicapped out of reason, spirits at the ebb
bear up; strung taut – by what volition keyed — as best they may.
    As grievous invalids watch the returning light pale-bright the
ruckled counterpane, see their uneased bodies only newly clear;
fearful to know afresh their ill condition; yet made glad for that
rising, yet strain ears to the earliest note — should some prevenient
bird make his kindly cry.
    Chance modulations in the fluxing mist, retro-fold roll, banked
up — shield again the waking arborage.
    With the gaining spread grey proto-light,
Morning-star pallid,
with the freshing day,
billowed damp more thickly hung yet whitened marvellously.
    Nothing was defined beyond where the ground steepened just in
front, where the trip-wire graced its snare-barbs with tinselled
moistnesses.
    Cloying drift-damp cupped in every concave place.
    It hurts you in the bloody eyes, it grips chill and harmfully and
rasps the sensed membrane of the throat; it's raw cold, it makes you
sneeze – christ how cold it is.
    With each moment passing — the opaque creeping into every
crevice creeping, whiter — thick whitened, through-white, argent
wall nebulous, took on, gave back, wholly reflected — till transfigured
bright in each drenched dew particle — and the last Night-Sentry
fidgets expectantly.
    Keep on that fire-step.
    Keep a sharp look out.
    Sights down — watch the wire.
    Keep your eyes skinned — it's a likely morning.
    Behind them, beyond the brumous piling the last stars paled
and twinkled fitfully, then faded altogether; knowing the mastery
and their visitation; this beautiful one, his cloud garments dyed,

ruddy-flecked, fleecy-stoled; the bright healer, climbing certainly the exact degrees to his meridian. Yet the brume holds, defiantly, and with winter confident, to shroud the low places.

Even now you couldn't see his line, but it was much lighter. The wire-tangle hanging, the rank grass-tangle drenched, tousled, and the broken-tin glint showed quite clearly. Left and right in the fire-bays you could see: soft service-caps wet-moulded to their heads moving — their drawn upward cloth flaps like home-spun angler-heads — moving in the morning reaches.

Very slowly the dissipating mist reveals saturate green-grey flats, and dark up-jutting things; and pollard boles by more than timely wood-craftsman's cunning pruning dockt, — these weeping willows shorn.

And the limber-wheel, whose fractured spokes search upward vainly for the rent-off mortised-rim.

Now his wire thickets were visible as dark surf, before a strand rising to bleached wall of bags in neat layers. The light of day is fully master now, and all along, and from beyond the glistering wall, at irregular intervals, thin blue smoke rises straight, like robber-fire, to thin-out amber against the eastern bright.

Over Biez Copse, as nainsook, low vapours yet could draw out tenuous parallels.

21.

Who is the great one who goes over earth,
Devouring water and wood?
He fears no warrior but wind he dreads,
And his sworn foe is the sun.   (*Fog*)

22.

Has the reader any distinct idea of what clouds are?

That mist which lies in the morning so softly in the valley, level and white, through which the tops of the trees rise as if through an inundation – why is *it* so heavy? and why does it lie so low, being yet so thin and frail that it will melt away utterly into splendour of morning, when the sun has shone on it but a few moments more? Those colossal pyramids, huge and firm, with outlines as of rocks, and strength to bear the beating of the high sun full on their fiery flanks – why are *they* so light, – their bases high over our heads, high over the heads of Alps? Why will these melt away, not as the sun *rises*, but as he *descends*, and leave the stars of twilight clear; while the valley vapour gains again upon the earth, like a shroud?

Or that ghost of a cloud, which steals by yonder clump of pines; nay, which does *not* steal by them, but haunts them, wreathing yet round them, and yet – and yet – slowly; now falling in a fair waved line like a woman's veil; now fading, now gone; we look away for an instant, and look back, and it is again there. What has it to do with that clump of pines, that it broods by them, and weaves itself among their branches, to and fro? Has it hidden a cloudy treasure among the moss at their roots, which it watches thus? Or has some strong enchanter charmed it into fond returning, or bound it fast within those bars of bough? And yonder filmy crescent, bent like an archer's bow above the snowy summit, the highest of all the hills, – that white arch which never forms but over the supreme crest – how is it stayed there, repelled apparently from the snow – nowhere touching it, the clear sky seen between it and the mountain edge, yet never leaving it – poised as a white bird hovers over its nest? (...)

Our business in this chapter, then, is with the upper clouds, which, owing to their quietness and multitude, we may perhaps conveniently think of as the 'cloud-flocks'. And we have to discover if any laws of beauty attach to them, such as we have seen in mountains or tree-branches.

23.

Yes I remember when the changeful earth
And twice five seasons on my mind had stamp'd
The faces of the moving year, even then,
A child, I held unconscious intercourse
With the eternal Beauty, drinking in
A pure organic pleasure from the lines
Of curling mist, or from the level plain
Of waters colour'd by the steady clouds.

24.

This morning, when it was time to rise, there was but a glimmering of daylight, and we had candles on the breakfast-table at nearly ten o'clock. All abroad there was a dense dim fog brooding through the atmosphere, in so much that we could hardly see across the street. At eleven o'clock I went out into the midst of the fog-bank, which for the moment seemed a little more interfused with daylight; for there seem to be continual changes in the density of this dim medium, which varies so much that now you can but just see your hand before you, and a moment afterwards you can see the cabs dashing out of the duskiness a score of yards off. It is seldom or never, moreover, an unmitigated gloom, but appears to be mixed up with sunshine in different proportions; sometimes only one part sun to a thousand of smoke and fog, and sometimes sunshine enough to give the whole mass a coppery hue. This would have been a bright sunny day but for the interference of the fog; and before I had been out long, I actually saw the sun looking red and rayless, much like the millionth magnification of a new halfpenny (…)

I went home by way of Holborn, and the fog was denser than ever, very black, indeed, more like a distillation of mud than anything else; the ghost of mud, the spiritualised medium of departed mud, through which the dead citizens of London probably tread, in the Hades whither they are translated. So heavy was the gloom, that gas was lighted in all the shop-windows; and the little charcoal-furnaces of the women and boys, roasting chestnuts, threw a ruddy, misty glow around them. And yet I liked it. This fog seems an atmosphere proper to huge, grimy London; as proper to London, as that light neither of the sun nor moon is to the New Jerusalem. On reaching home, I found the same fog diffused through the drawing-room, though how it could have got in is a mystery.

25.

… the months of amazement which followed my return to England – I was so ignorant, I never guessed when the great fogs fell that trains could take me to light and sunshine a few miles outside London. Once I faced the reflection of my own face in the jet-black mirror of the window-panes for five days. When the fog thinned, I looked out and saw a man standing opposite the pub where the barmaid lived. Of a sudden his breast turned dull red like a robin's, and he crumpled, having cut his throat. In a few minutes – seconds it seemed – a hand-ambulance arrived and took up the body. A pot-boy with a bucket of steaming water sluiced the blood off into the gutter, and what little crowd had collected went its way.

26.

The sun was still concealed below the opposite hilltops, though it was shining already, not twenty feet above my head, on our own mountain slope. But the scene, beyond a few near features, was entirely changed. Napa Valley was gone; gone were all the lower slopes and woody foothills of the range; and in their place, not a thousand feet below me, rolled a great level ocean. It was as though I had gone to bed the night before, safe in a nook of inland mountains and had awakened in a bay upon the coast. I had seen these inundations from below; at Calistoga I had risen and gone abroad in the early morning, coughing and sneezing, under fathoms and fathoms of grey sea vapour, like a cloudy sky – a dull sight for the artist, and a painful experience for the invalid. But to sit aloft one's self in the pure air and under the unclouded dome of heaven, and thus look down on the submergence of the valley, was strangely different and even delightful to the eyes. Far away were hilltops like little islands. Nearer, a smoky surf beat about the foot of the precipices and poured into all the coves of these rough mountains. The colour of that fog ocean was a thing never to be forgotten. For an instant, among the Hebrides and just about sundown, I have seen something like it on the sea itself. But the white was not so opaline; nor was there, what surprisingly increased the effect, that breathless crystal stillness over all. Even in its gentlest moods the salt sea travails, moaning among the weeds or lisping on the sand; but that vast fog ocean lay in a trance of silence, nor did the sweet air of the morning tremble with a sound.

As I continued to sit upon the dump, I began to observe that this sea was not so level as at first sight it appeared to be. Away in the extreme south, a little hill of fog arose against the sky above the general surface, and as it had already caught the sun it shone on the horizon like the topsails of some giant ship. There were huge waves, stationary, as it seemed, like waves in a frozen sea; and yet, as I looked again, I was not sure but they were moving after all, with a slow and august advance. And while I was yet doubting, a promontory of the hills some four or five miles away, conspicuous by a bouquet of tall pines, was in a single instant overtaken and swallowed up. It reappeared in a little, with its pines, but this time as an islet and only to be swallowed up once more and then for good. This set me looking nearer, and I saw that in every cove along the line of mountains the fog was being piled in higher and higher, as though by some wind that was inaudible to me. I could trace its progress, one pine tree first growing hazy and then disappearing after another; although sometimes there was none of this forerunning haze, but the whole opaque white ocean gave a start and swallowed a piece of mountain at a gulp. It was to flee these poisonous fogs that I had left the seaboard, and climbed so high among the mountains. And now, behold, here came the fog to besiege me in my chosen altitudes, and yet came so beautifully that my first thought was of welcome.

27.

CYRIL.   The theory is certainly a very curious one, but to make it complete you must show that Nature, no less than Life, is an imitation of Art. Are you prepared to prove that ?
VIVIAN.   My dear fellow, I am prepared to prove anything.
CYRIL.   Nature follows the landscape painter then, and takes her effects from him?
VIVIAN.   Certainly. Where, if not from the Impressionists, do we get those wonderful brown fogs that come creeping down our streets, blurring the gas-lamps and changing the houses into monstrous shadows? To whom, if not to them and their master, do we owe the lovely silver mists that brood over our river, and turn to faint forms of fading grace curved bridge and swaying barge? The extraordinary change that has taken place in the climate of London during the last ten years is entirely due to this particular school of Art. You smile. Consider the matter from a scientific or a metaphysical point of view, and you will find that I am right. For what is Nature? Nature is no

great mother who has borne us. She is our creation. It is in our brain that she quickens to life. Things are because we see them, and what we see, and how we see it, depends on the Arts that have influenced us. To look at a thing is very different from seeing a thing. One does not see anything until one sees its beauty. Then, and then only, does it come into existence. At present, people see fogs, not because there are fogs, but because poets and painters have taught them the mysterious loveliness of such effects. There may have been fogs for centuries in London. I dare say there were. But no one saw them, and so we do not know anything about them. They did not exist till Art had invented them. Now, it must be admitted, fogs are carried to excess.

They have become the mere mannerism of a clique, and the exaggerated realism of their method gives dull people bronchitis. Where the cultured catch an effect, the uncultured catch cold. And so, let us be humane, and invite Art to turn her wonderful eyes elsewhere. She has done so already, indeed. That white quivering sunlight that one sees now in France, with its strange blotches of mauve, and its restless violet shadows, is her latest fancy, and, on the whole, Nature reproduces it quite admirably. Where she used to give us Corots and Daubignys, she gives us now exquisite Monets and entrancing Pissarros. Indeed there are moments, rare, it is true, but still to be observed from time to time, when Nature becomes absolutely modern. Of course she is not always to be relied upon. The fact is that she is in this unfortunate position. Art creates an incomparable and unique effect, and, having done so, passes on to other things. Nature, upon the other hand, forgetting that imitation can be made the sincerest form of insult, keeps on repeating this effect until we all become absolutely wearied of it. Nobody of any real culture, for instance, ever talks nowadays about the beauty of a sunset. Sunsets are quite old-fashioned. They belong to the time when Turner was the last note in art. To admire them is a distinct sign of provincialism of temperament. Upon the other hand they go on. Yesterday evening Mrs. Arundel insisted on my coming to the window, and looking at the glorious sky, as she called it. Of course I had to look at it. She is one of those absurdly pretty Philistines, to whom one can deny nothing. And what was it ? It was simply a very second-rate Turner, a Turner of a bad period, with all the painter's worst faults exaggerated and overemphasized.

28.

For some moments ... I remained closeted with the little person inside me, the melodious psalmist of the rising sun, of whom I have already spoken. Of the different persons who compose our personality, it is not the most obvious that are the most essential. In myself, when ill health has succeeded in uprooting them one after another, there will still remain two or three endowed with a hardier constitution than the rest – notably a certain philosopher who is happy only when he has discovered between two works of art, between two sensations, a common element. But I have sometimes wondered whether the last of all might not be this little mannikin, very similar to another whom the optician at Combray used to set up in his shop window to forecast the weather, and who, doffing his hood when the sun shone, would put it on again if it was going to rain. I know how selfish this little mannikin is; I may be suffering from an attack of breathlessness which only the coming of rain would assuage, but he pays no heed, and, at the first drops so impatiently awaited, all his gaiety forgotten, he sullenly pulls down his hood. Conversely, I dare say that in my last agony, when all my other 'selves' are dead, if a ray of sunshine steals into the room while I am drawing my last breath, the little barometric mannikin will feel a great relief, and will throw back his hood to sing: 'Ah, fine weather at last!'

29.

The rain never catches them without warning. Either as it gathers, the cranes fly up out of the valleys; or a calf looks up at the sky and sniffs the winds with wide nostrils; or the shrill swallow flies round and round the lake and the frogs chant their old grievance in the mud; or more often, the ant, beating a tiny track, carries her eggs up from her underground house and the great rainbow stoops to drink and armies of rooks leaving the fields in long columns clatter their crowded wings; all kinds of sea-birds and birds of freshwater pools who hunt the flood-plains of the Cayster, you can see them bickering and splashing their backs, now dipping their heads in the current, now running at the waves and fooling about in their bathing; then with her deep voice the raven summons the rain, evil and alone she paces the dry sand.

Not even girls, finishing their night-work, can ignore the coming
storm, when they see the oil flare up in their lamp and the mould-
patches growing.

30.

Our farms are in the patched blue overlap
between Queensland rain and Victorian rain
(and of two-faced droughts like a dustbowl tap).

The southerly rain is skimmed and curled
off the Roaring Forties' circuit of the world.
It is our chased Victorian silver

and makes wintry asphalt hurry on the spot
or pauses to a vague speed in the air,
whereas, lightning-brewed in a vast coral pot

the tropical weather disgorges its lot
in days of enveloping floodtime blast
towering and warm as a Papuan forest,

a rain you can sweat in, it steams in the sun
like a hard-ridden horse, while southern rain's absorbed
like a cool, fake-colloquial, drawn out lesson.

31.

You remember that village where the border ran
Down the middle of the street,
With the butcher and baker in different states?
Today he remarked how a shower of rain

Had stopped so cleanly across Golightly's lane
It might have been a wall of glass
That had toppled over. He stood there, for ages,
To wonder which side, if any, he should be on.

32.

'The purpose of language is to express thoughts.' So presumably the purpose of every sentence is to express a thought. Then what thought is expressed, for example, by the sentence 'It is raining'?

*

Consider the misbegotten sentence 'It may be raining, but isn't.' And here one should be on one's guard against saying that 'It may be raining' really means 'I think it'll be raining'. For why not the other way round, why should not the latter mean the former? Do not regard a hesitant assertion as an assertion of hesitancy.

*

Can I say 'bububu' and mean 'If it doesn't rain I shall go for a walk'? – It is only in a language that I can mean something by something.

*

We might very well write every statement in the form of a question followed by a 'Yes'; for instance: 'Is it raining? Yes!' Would this show that every statement contained a question?

33.

— Pray what was that man's name, — for I write in such a hurry, I have no time to recollect or look for it, — who first made the observation, 'That there was great inconstancy in our air and climate'? Whoever he was, 'twas a just and good observation in him. — But the corollary drawn from it, namely, 'That it is this which has furnished us with such a variety of odd and whimsical characters'; — that was not his; — it was found out by another man, at least a century and a half after him: — Then again, — that this copious store-house of original materials, is the true and natural cause that our Comedies are so much better than those of *France*, or any others that either have, or can be wrote upon the Continent; — that discovery was not fully made till about the middle of king *William's* reign, — when the great *Dryden*, in writing one of his long prefaces, (if I mistake not) most fortunately hit upon it. Indeed towards the latter end of queen *Anne*, the great *Addison* began to patronize the notion, and more fully explained it to the world in one or two of his Spectators; — but the discovery was not his. — Then, fourthly and lastly, that this strange irregularity in our climate, producing so strange an irregularity in our characters, — doth thereby, in some sort, make us amends, by giving us somewhat to make us merry with when the weather will not suffer us to go out of doors, — that observation is my own; — and was struck out by me this very rainy day, March 26, 1759, and betwixt the hours of nine and ten in the morning.

34.

DOYLE.   My dear Tom, you only need a touch of the Irish climate to be as big a fool as I am myself … Go and marry the most English Englishwoman you can find, and then bring up your son in Rosscullen; and that son's character will be so like mine and so unlike yours that everybody will accuse me of being his father. [*With sudden anguish*] Rosscullen! oh good Lord, Rosscullen! The dullness! the hopelessness! the ignorance! the bigotry!

BROADBENT.   [*matter-of-factly*]. The usual thing in the country, Larry. Just the same here.

DOYLE.   [*hastily*]. No, no: the climate is different. Here, if the life is dull, you can be dull too, and no great harm done. [*Going off into a passionate dream*] But your wits can't thicken in that soft moist air, on those white springy roads, in those misty rushes and brown bogs, on those hillsides of granite rocks and magenta heather. You've no such colours in the sky, no such lure in the distances, no such sadness in the evenings. Oh, the dreaming! the dreaming! the torturing, heartscalding, never satisfying dreaming, dreaming, dreaming, dreaming! [*Savagely*] No debauchery that ever coarsened and brutalized an Englishman can take the worth and usefulness out of him like that dreaming.

35.

Very large houses suddenly collapsed. Small houses remained standing.

A fat hard egg-shaped orange-cloud suddenly hung over the town. It seemed to hang on the pointed point of the steep spindly town hall tower and radiated violet.

A dry, naked tree stretched its quaking and quivering long branches into the deep sky. It was very black, like a hole in white paper. Its four little leaves quivered for a long time. But there was no sign of wind. But when the storm came and buildings with thick walls fell down, the thin branches didn't move. The little leaves turned stiff: as if cast out of iron.

A flock of crows flew through the air in a straight line over the town.

And suddenly again everything was still.

The orange-cloud disappeared. The sky turned piercing blue. The town yellow enough to make you cry. And through this silence a single sound rang: hoofbeats. And they knew that through the totally empty streets a white horse is walking all alone.

The sound lasted for a long time, a very, very long time. So no one knew exactly when it disappeared. Who knows when silence begins?

Through elongated, extended, somewhat expressionless, unsympathetic notes of a bassoon rolling far, far away deep in the distant emptiness, everything slowly turned green. First low and rather dirty. Then brighter and brighter, colder and colder, poisonous and more poisonous, even brighter, even colder, even more poisonous.

The buildings soared upward and became narrower. All of them leaned toward a point to the right, where perhaps the morning is.

It became perceptible as a striving toward morning.

And the sky, the houses, the pavement and the people who walked on the pavement became brighter, colder, more poisonously green. The people walked constantly, continually, slowly, always staring straight ahead. And always alone.

But the naked tree correspondingly grew a large, luxurious crown. This crown sat up high and had a compact, sausage-like shape that curved upward. The crown alone was so shrilly yellow that no soul would endure it.

It's good that none of the people walking below saw this crown.

Only the bassoon attempted to describe the colour. It rose higher and higher, became shrill and nasal in its outstretched note.

How good that the bassoon couldn't reach this note.

36.

For six days and six nights the winds blew, torrent and tempest and flood overwhelmed the world, tempest and flood raged together like warring hosts. When the seventh day dawned the storm from the south subsided, the sea grew calm, the flood was stilled; I looked at the face of the world and there was silence, all mankind was turned to clay. The surface of the sea stretched as flat as a rooftop; I opened a hatch and the light fell on my face. Then I bowed low, I sat down and I wept, the tears streamed down my face, for on every side was the waste of water. I looked for land in vain, but fourteen leagues distant there appeared a mountain, and there the boat grounded.

37.

Rain patters on a sea that tilts and sighs.
Fast-running floors, collapsing into hollows,
Tower suddenly, spray-haired. Contrariwise,

A wave drops like a wall: another follows,
Wilting and scrambling, tirelessly at play
Where there are no ships and no shallows.

Above the sea, the yet more shoreless day,
Riddled by wind, trails lit-up galleries:
They shift to giant ribbing, sift away.

Such attics cleared of me! Such absences!

38.

The surgeon in question was carrying out this operation and talking
his assistant through the anatomy, when he suddenly stopped in
mid-stream and asked the whole team to gather around the patient on
his side of the table. The fact that the invitation was so cordial took
some of the team by surprise, as they dutifully moved closer. The
surgeon had gently lifted a portion of the intestine to reveal some
fascia (connective tissue). A combination of the reflective surface from
the liquidity of the tissue illuminated by surgical lights was producing
an extraordinary local rainbow effect. The gut fascia was shimmering.
The surgeon wanted to share with the team this moment of wonder,
the revelation, or perhaps the conjuring, of this interior rainbow ...

39.

IRIS.   Ceres, most bounteous Lady, thy rich Leas
Of Wheate, Rye, Barley, Vetches, Oates and Pease;
Thy Turfie Mountaines, where live nibling Sheepe,
And flat Meads thatch'd with Stover, them to keepe;
Thy banks with pionèd and twillèd brims,
Which spungie *Aprill* at thy hest betrims,
To make cold Nymphs chaste crownes; & thy broome-groves,
Whose shadow the dismissed Bachelor loves,
Being lass-lorn; thy pole-clipt vineyard;
And thy sea-marge sterile and rocky-hard,
Where thou thyself dost ayre, the Queene o' the Skie,

Whose wat'ry Arch, and messenger, am I,
Bids thee leave these, & with her soveraign grace,

Juno descends.

Here on this grasse-plot, in this very place
To come and sport: her Peacocks fly amaine:
Approach, rich *Ceres*, her to entertaine.

enter Ceres.

CERES.   Haile, many-colour'd Messenger, that ne'er
Dost disobey the wife of *Jupiter*;
Who with thy saffron wings upon my flowres
Diffusest honey drops, refreshing showres,
And with each end of thy blue bowe dost crowne
My boskie acres, and my unshrub'd downe,
Rich scarf to my proud earth; why hath thy Queene
Summon'd me hither, to this short-grass'd Greene?

40.

The day after a typhoon is extremely moving, and full of interest. The
lattice and open-weave fences around the garden have been left in a
shambles; and the various garden plants are in a miserable state.
Great trees have been blown over, and the branches ripped off; it gives
you quite a shock to discover them lying there across the bush clover
and valerian. Leaves are carefully lodged in all the little spaces of the
lattice weave, so delicate an effect that you cannot imagine it was the
doing of the wild wind.

41.

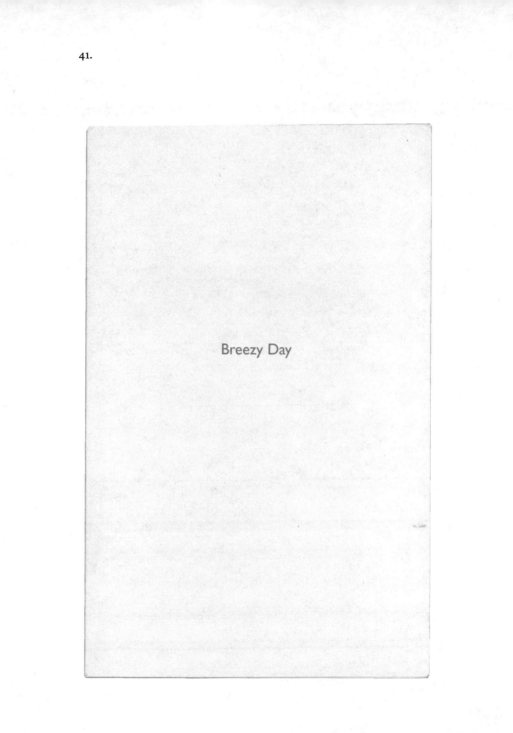

Breezy Day

42.

In truth, my Glass being opposite to the Window, I seldom shave without cutting myself. Some Mountain or Peak is rising out of the Mist, or some slanting Column of misty Sunlight is sailing across me, so that I offer up soap & blood daily, as an Eye-servant of the Goddess Nature.

43.

The poet must be continually watching the moods of his mind as the astronomer watches the aspects of the heavens. What might we not expect from a long life faithfully spent in this wise – the humblest observer would see some stars shoot. – A faithful description as by a disinterested person of the thoughts which visited a certain mind in three score years and ten, as when one reports the number and character of the vehicles which pass a particular point. As travellers go round the world and report natural objects & phenomena – so faithfully let another stay at home & report the phenomena of his own life. Catalogue stars – those thoughts whose orbits are as rarely calculated as comets. It matters not whether they visit my mind or yours – whether the meteor falls in my field or in yours – only that it came from heaven. (…) A meteorological journal of the mind – You shall observe what occurs in your latitude, I in mine.

44.

The more I study it, the more powerfully am I gripped by the nature of our native land. The thunderstorm, not only in its higher manifestations but as a prospect, power and shape, among the other forms taken by the skies; how light works, shaping national character as a principle and as a mode of destiny (so that something should be sacred to us), the way it moves as it comes and goes; the characteristics of the woods and the coming-together in one place of different kinds of nature, so that all the sacred places of the earth are condensed in one place; the philosophical light around my window – these are now my delight.

45.

Other herbs with spontaneous movement are less well-known; the Hedysarea, in particular, among which the *Hedysarum gyrans* or *swaying sainfoin*, which bestirs itself in a surprising way. This small leguminous plant, originally from Bengal but often grown in our hothouses, performs a kind of non-stop intricate dance in honor of the light. Its leaves divide themselves into three leaflets, one broad and terminal, the other two narrow and planted at the base of the first. Each of these leaflets has its own different movement. They live in incessant, rhythmical, and almost chronometrical agitation. They are so sensitive to light that their dance slows down or speeds up according to whether the clouds hide or reveal the chink of sky they face. They are, as we can see, true photometers, and this well before Crooke's invention of the natural otheoscope.

46.

Then she took out
her metal fan
which was like this:
On one side of the fan
were painted many pictures,
countless pictures
of frost-laden clouds.
On the other side of the fan
were painted
many pictures,
countless pictures
of summer rainstorms.
She took out this fan.
She pointed toward me
the part of the fan with pictures
of frost-laden clouds.
Slowly
she fluttered it in my direction.
As she did this,
a fierce winter sleet storm
came raining down.

Then I took out
my metal fan
and pointed toward her
the part of it with pictures
of the scorching rays of sunlight,
the lethal rays of sunlight. . .

47.

This morning the woman in the boulangerie said: 'It's still lovely, but the heat is lasting too long!' (people around here always feel that it's too lovely, too hot). I add: 'And the light is so beautiful!' But the woman does not answer, and again I notice that short-circuit in language of which the most trivial conversations are the sure occasion. I realize that *seeing the light* relates to a class sensibility; or rather, since there are 'picturesque' lights which are certainly enjoyed by the woman in the bakery, what is socially marked is the 'vague' view, the view without contours, without object, *without figuration*, the view of a transparency, the view of a non-view (that unfigurative value which occurs in good painting and never in bad). In short, nothing more cultural than the atmosphere, nothing more ideological than what the weather is doing.

48.

The cliché concerning the cliché of weather talk is that we talk about the weather as a way of avoiding talking about anything else, anything that would commit us to a point of view that might threaten the social bond for which weather talk is such a balm. When you stop to think about it, this is weird. Something important to your very sense of being, something beyond anybody's control, truly the wild beyond, namely, the weather, becomes hijacked as socializing grease for which grunts and groans might serve just as well. Hence Mark Twain's observation, 'Everybody's talking about the weather but nobody's doing anything about it.' Weather talk is like wind rustling through our bodies as acknowledgment of sociability. Weather talk is soft and sweet, acknowledging our alienation from nature no less than from one another, a relic of the superstition that to talk otherwise might rile it.

49.

This house has been far out at sea all night,
The woods crashing through darkness, the booming hills,
Winds stampeding the fields under the window
Floundering black astride and blinding wet

Till day rose; then under an orange sky
The hills had new places, and wind wielded
Blade-light, luminous black and emerald,
Flexing like the lens of a mad eye.

At noon I scaled along the house-side as far as
The coal-house door. Once I looked up –
Through the brunt wind that dented the balls of my eyes
The tent of the hills drummed and strained its guyrope,

The fields quivering, the skyline a grimace,
At any second to bang and vanish with a flap;
The wind flung a magpie away and a black-
Back gull bent like an iron bar slowly. The house

Rang like some fine green goblet in the note
That any second would shatter it. Now deep
In chairs, in front of the great fire, we grip
Our hearts and cannot entertain book, thought,

Or each other. We watch the fire blazing,
And feel the roots of the house move, but sit on,
Seeing the window tremble to come in,
Hearing the stones cry out under the horizons.

50.

All the leaves which hung towards the earth by the bending of the
shoots with their branches, are turned upside down by the gusts of
wind, and here their perspective is reversed; for, if the tree is between
you and the quarter of the wind, the leaves which are towards you

remain in their natural aspect, while those on the opposite side which ought to have their points in a contrary direction have, by being turned over, their points turned towards you.

51.

And now begin the doleful notes to reach me; now am I come where much lamenting strikes me.

I came into a place void of all light, which bellows like the sea in tempest, when it is combated by opposing winds.

The infernal hurricane that never rests, leads the spirits with its sweep; whirling them round and smiting it vexes them.

When they arrive before the ruin, there the shrieks, the moanings and the lamentations, there they blaspheme the divine power.

I learnt that to such torment are doomed the carnal sinners, who subject reason to lust.

And as the wings of starlings bear them along, in the cold season, in large and crowded troop, so doth that blast the evil spirits.

Hither thither downward upward it leads them. No hope ever comforts them, not of repose but even of lesser pain.

And as the cranes go chanting their lays, making a long streak of themselves in the air; so I saw the shadows coming, uttering wails

borne onward by that strife of winds; whereupon I said: Master, who are those people, whom the black air lashes so?

(…)

Helen is there, for whom so many years of ill revolved; and see the great Achilles, who fought at the last with love;

see Paris, Tristan; and more than a thousand shades he showed me, and pointing with his finger, named to me those whom love had dispatched from our life.

After I had listened to my teacher naming the dames of old and cavaliers, pity came over me and I was as if bewildered.

I began: O Poet, willingly would I speak with those two who go together and seem so light upon the wind.

And he to me: Thou shalt see, when they are nearer to us; and then do thou entreat them by that love which leads them and they will come.

Soon as the wind in our direction bends them, I raised my voice: Oh wearied souls! Come and speak to us, if none denies it.

As turtle doves, called onward by desire, with raised and steady wings come through the air to their sweet nest, borne by their will,

so those spirits separated from the band where Dido is, approaching us through the malign air, such was the force of my affectionate cry.

Oh living creature gracious and benign! that goest through the black air, visiting us who stained the earth with blood:

if the king of the universe were our friend, we would pray him to give thee peace, since thou hast pity on our perverse woe.

Of what it pleases thee to hear and speak, that will we hear, and speak with you, whilst the wind, as now, is silent for us.

52.

To men the winds are as wings. For by them men are borne and fly, not indeed through the air but over the sea; a vast gate of commerce is opened, and the whole world is rendered accessible. To the earth, which is the seat and habitation of men, they serve for brooms, sweeping and cleansing both it and the air itself. Yet they damage the character of the sea, which would otherwise be calm and harmless; and in other respects they are productive of mischief. Without any human agency they cause strong and violent motion; whence they are as hired servants to drive ships and turn mills, and may, if human industry fail not, be employed for many other purposes. The nature of the winds is generally ranked among the things mysterious and concealed; and no wonder, when the power and nature of the air, which the winds attend and serve (as represented by the poets in the relation of Aeolus to Juno), is entirely unknown. They are not primary creatures, nor among the works of the six days; as neither are the other meteors actually; but produced according to the order of creation.

53.

In a mountainous region where day in and day out one hears the wind relentlessly execute the same unvarying theme, one is perhaps tempted for a moment to ignore the inadequacy of the analogy and rejoice in this symbol of the consistency and assurance of human freedom. We do not perhaps reflect that there was a moment when the wind, which for so many years has had its dwelling-place among these mountains, came to this region as a stranger, and flung itself wildly, meaninglessly through the canyons, down into the caverns, producing now a piercing shriek by which it almost startled itself, now a hollow roar from which it had itself to flee, now a note of lamentation, without knowing why; then a sigh drawn from the anguish of the abyss, so profound that the wind itself was for a moment afraid and doubted that it dared to dwell in these regions; then a gay and lyrical waltz of gladness – until, having learnt to know its instrument, the wind worked all of this into the melody which from day to day it performs unchangeably. So too does the individual's possibility wander among its own possibilities, discovering now one and now another.

54.

We reached Aiolia, where Hippotas' son
Aiolos beloved of the immortal gods,
lived on a floating island. Right round it ran
sheer cliffs and a wall of unbreakable bronze.
There were twelve children in his home,
six daughters and six youthful sons,
and he'd given his daughters to the sons as wives.
They always dine together with their mother
and father on lavish food of every kind.
By day the house is filled with savoury steam
and flute-music; at night they sleep, each beside
his wife, in fine bedding on decorated beds.
It was their town, their lovely home we came to.
For a month in all, the chief hosted me and asked
about the fleet, Troy, the Akhaians' return,
and I narrated everything in order.
When I asked to continue on my way,
to be sent off, he did not refuse, but sent me.
He gave me a bag, made from flayed ox-hide
and bound inside the ways of the blustering winds;
for Zeus had made him keeper of the winds,
able to stop them all at will, or make them blow.
On board, he tied this bag with a shining
silver cord, so not the least breeze could escape,
and sent a westerly wind to blow for me,
to convey my ships and men. All in vain –
our own mad folly brought us to disaster.

  We sailed nine days and nights. Already
on the tenth day our native land appeared
and we saw people nearby making fires.
Then, in my exhaustion, sweet sleep took me
(to reach home quicker, I'd handled the sails
all the way and let no other guide them).
But now my comrades murmured to each other
that I was bringing gold and silver home,
gifts from Hippotas' son, great Aiolos.

  Each, glancing at his neighbour said:

'It's wrong! Whatever town or land we come to,
all men honour our chief and make him welcome.
He has on board great wealth from the spoils of Troy,
yet we, on our side, who travelled the same road
must come home empty-handed. And Aiolos
now, as a friendly guest-gift, has given him
all this. But come, let's quickly look and see
how much silver and gold are in the bag.'
　　　　So they spoke, and their bad idea prevailed.
They opened the bag – all the winds burst out
and the squall bore them, weeping, out across
the ocean, away from their native soil.
Then I awoke, and pondered in my heart
whether to throw myself overboard and drown,
or to stay alive in silence and endure.
I kept silent and endured; wrapped in my cloak
I lay there. My men groaned as the raging squall
bore the ships back to the island of Aiolia.

55.

Empedocles has been admired on many grounds. For instance, when
the Etesian winds once began to blow violently and to damage the
crops, he ordered asses to be flayed and bags to be made of their skin.
These he stretched out here and there on the hills and headlands to
catch the wind and, because this checked the wind, he was called the
'stayer of winds'.

56.

That a King-fisher hanged by the bill, sheweth in what quarter the
wind is by an occult and secret propriety, converting the breast to that
point of the Horizon from whence the wind doth blow, is a received
opinion, and very strange; introducing natural Weather-cocks, and
extending Magnetical positions as far as Animal Natures. A conceit
supported chiefly by present practice, yet not made out by Reason or
Experience.

Unto Reason it seemeth very repugnant, that a carcass or body disanimated, should be so affected with every wind, as to carry a conformable respect and constant habitude thereto. For although in sundry Animals we deny not a kind of natural Meteorology or innate presention both of wind and weather, yet that proceeding from sense receiving impressions from the first mutation of the air, they cannot in reason retain that apprehension after death, as being affections which depend on life, and depart upon disanimation. And therefore with more favourable Reason may we draw the same effect or sympathie upon the Hedg-hog, whose presention of winds is so exact, that it stoppeth the North or Southern hole of its nest, according to the prenotion of these winds ensuing; which some men observing, have been able to make predictions which way the wind would turn, and been esteemed hereby wise men in point of weather. Now this proceeding from sense in the creature alive, it were not reasonable to hang up an Hedg-hogs head, and to expect a conformable motion unto its living conversion.

... As for experiment, we cannot make it out by any we have attempted; for if a single King-fisher be hanged up with untwisted silk in an open room, and where the air is free, it observes not a constant respect unto the mouth of the wind, but variously converting, doth seldom breast it right. If two be suspended in the same room, they will not regularly conform their breasts, but oft-times respect the opposite points of Heaven. And if we conceive that for exact exploration, they should be suspended where the air is quiet and unmoved, that clear of impediments, they may more freely convert upon their natural verticity; we have also made this way of inquisition, suspending them in large and capacious glasses closely stopped; wherein nevertheless we observed a casual station, and that they rested irregularly upon conversion...

The ground of this popular practice might be the common opinion concerning the vertue prognostick of these Birds; as also the natural regard they have unto the winds, and they unto them again; more especially remarkable in the time of their nidulation, and bringing forth their young. For at that time, which happeneth about the brumal Solstice, it hath been observed even unto a proverb, that the Sea is calm, and the winds do cease, till the young ones are excluded; and forsake their nest which floateth upon the Sea, and by the roughness of winds might otherwise be overwhelmed.

57.

CHORUS.   It is from us, the birds, that Man receives all his greatest blessings. From us he learns of the coming of spring, of winter, of autumn. The cry of the crane as it flies back to Libya tells him it is the season for sowing; the shipmaster knows that he can hang up his rudder and enjoy a good night's rest; Orestes weaves himself a warm winter cloak – no point in freezing to death while he's on his way to steal someone else's. But when the kite appears, another season is at hand. Time for the sheep-shearing! Spring is here! Then comes the swallow: time to sell those warm woollen clothes and buy something more summery.

58.

July 1872 – Nov 8. Walking with Wm Splaine we saw a vast multitude of starlings making an unspeakable jangle. They would settle in a row of trees; then, one tree after another, rising at a signal they looked like a cloud of specks of black snuff or powder struck up from a brush or broom or shaken from a wig; then they would sweep round in whirlwinds – you could see the nearer and farther bow of the rings by the size and blackness; many would be in one phase at once, all narrow black flakes hurling round, then in another; then they would fall upon a field and so on … stirring and cheering one another.

59.

November 27, 1799 – I saw Starlings in vast Flights, borne along like smoke, mist – like a body unindued with voluntary Power – now it shaped itself into a circular area, inclined – now they formed a Square – now a Globe – now from complete Orb into an Ellipse – then oblongated into a Balloon with the Car suspended, now a concave Semicircle; still expanding, or contracting, thinning or condensing, now glimmering and shivering, now thickening, deepening, blackening!

60.

We are accustomed to say in New England that few and fewer pigeons visit us every year. Our forests furnish no mast for them. So, it would seem, few and fewer thoughts visit each growing man from year to year, for the grove in our minds is laid waste.

61.

When an individual is seen gliding through the woods and close to the observer, it passes like a thought, and on trying to see it again, the eye searches in vain; the bird is gone.

The multitudes of wild pigeons in our woods are astonishing. Indeed, after having viewed them so often, and under so many circumstances, I even now feel inclined to pause and assure myself that what I am going to relate is fact. Yet I have seen it all, and that too in the company of persons who, like myself, were struck with amazement.

In the autumn of 1813, I left my house at Henderson, on the banks of the Ohio River, on my way to Louisville. In passing over the Barrens a few miles beyond Hardensburgh, I observed the pigeons flying from northeast to southwest in greater numbers than I thought I had ever seen them before, and feeling an inclination to count the flocks that might pass within the reach of my eye in one hour, I dismounted, seated myself on an eminence, and began to mark with my pencil, making a dot for every flock that passed. In a short time finding the task which I had undertaken impracticable, as the birds poured in in countless multitudes, I rose and, counting the dots then put down, found that 163 had been made in twenty-one minutes. I travelled on, and still met more the farther I proceeded. The air was literally filled with pigeons; the light of noon-day was obscured as by an eclipse; the dung fell in spots, not unlike melting flakes of snow, and the continued buzz of wings had a tendency to lull my senses to repose . . .

When a hawk chanced to press upon the rear of a flock – at once, like a torrent, and with a noise like thunder, they rushed into a compact mass, pressing upon each other towards the centre. In these almost solid masses, they darted forward in undulating and

angular lines, descended and swept close over the earth with
inconceivable velocity, mounted perpendicularly so as to resemble a
vast column, and, when high, were seen wheeling and twisting
within their continued lines, which then resembled the coils of a
gigantic serpent.

62.

There are birds on the water,
birds in the air,
on the snags, in the conifers,
birds flying down to the lakefloor,
and birds on the ice, half a million years old,
that is melting away at the foot of the world.

There are birds in the air,
birds on the water.
There are birds who are building invisible, audible nests
in the bare-naked limbs of the alders in winter,
birds on the ground, overturning the layers
of last summer's leaves.

There are birds stropping their beaks
on your half-curled fingers.
They perch on your shoulders,
store food in your ears
and bring mosses and twigs
to your half-zippered pockets and palms.

Birds break their necks
flying into your eyes
in the perfect belief
that the brilliant interior world
is as spacious and seamless and real
as the world outside.

There are birds on the water,
birds in the air,

and birds lying dead at your feet,
who had never once feared
that your eyes might not mean what they're seeing,
your mind might not mean what it hears.

There are birds in the air,
birds on the water,
but no birds in heaven
and no birds in hell
and no one to tell them the difference,
not here and not there.

63.

One time before the Plague was begun (otherwise than as I have said
in St. *Giles's*), I think it was in *March*, seeing a Crowd of People in
the Street, I join'd with them to satisfy my Curiosity, and found them
all staring up into the Air, to see what a Woman told them appeared
plain to her, which was an Angel cloth'd in white, with a fiery Sword
in his Hand, waving it, or brandishing it over his Head. She
described every Part of the Figure to the Life; shew'd them the
Motion, and the Form; and the poor People came into it so eagerly,
and with so much Readiness; *YES, I see it all plainly*, says one. *There's
the Sword as plain as can be.* Another saw the Angel. One saw his
very Face, and cry'd out, What a glorious Creature he was! One saw
one thing, and one another. I look'd as earnestly as the rest, but,
perhaps, with not so much Willingness to be impos'd upon; and I
said, indeed, that *I could see nothing*, but a white Cloud, bright on
one Side, by the shining of the Sun upon the other Part. The woman
endeavour'd to shew it me, but could not make me confess, that I
saw it, which, indeed, if I had, I must have lied: But the woman
turning upon me, look'd in my Face, and fancied I laugh'd, in which
her Imagination deceiv'd her too; for I really did not laugh, but was
very seriously reflecting how the poor People were terrified, by the
Force of their own Imagination. However, she turn'd from me, call'd
me profane Fellow, and a Scoffer; told me, that it was a time of God's
Anger, and dreadful Judgments were approaching; and that
Despisers, such as, I should *wander and perish.*

64.

A Klee painting named 'Angelus Novus' shows an angel looking as though he is about to move away from something he is fixedly contemplating. His eyes are staring, his mouth is open, his wings are spread. This is how one pictures the angel of history. His face is turned toward the past. Where we perceive a chain of events, he sees one single catastrophe which keeps piling wreckage upon wreckage and hurls it in front of his feet. The angel would like to stay, awaken the dead, and make whole what has been smashed. But a storm is blowing from Paradise; it has got caught in his wings with such violence that the angel can no longer close them. This storm irresistibly propels him into the future to which his back is turned, while the pile of debris before him grows skyward. This storm is what we call progress.

65.

We naturally admire things that are above us, such as celestial phenomena or the clouds. Although they are only a little higher than the mountains, and one sees them, often indeed, lower than the tops of our bell towers, because we must look up to see them, painters and poets depict them as the throne of God, and show Him using his own hands to open and close the doors of the winds, to sprinkle rain upon the flowers and hurl lightning on the rocks. This makes me hope that if I explain here the nature of clouds, so that no longer will you merely wonder at what you see, or what falls from above, in the same way you will consider it possible to discover the causes of all that is most wonderful on the earth (…) I hope that those who have understood everything spoken of in this treatise in the future will not see anything in the clouds whose causes cannot be easily understood or that would be cause for wonder.

66.

In order to understand the indications of the weather, they studied the clouds according to the classification of Luke Howard. They stared at those which spread out like manes, those which resemble islands, and those which might be taken for mountains of snow – trying to distinguish nimbus from cirrus and stratus from cumulus. But the shapes had altered even before they could find the names. The barometer deceived them; the thermometer taught them nothing; and they had recourse to the device invented in the time of Louis XIV by a priest from Touraine. A leech in a glass bottle was to rise up in the event of rain, to stick to the bottom in settled weather, and to move about if a storm were threatening. But nearly always the atmosphere contradicted the leech. Three others were put in along with it. All four behaved differently.

67.

The principal Modifications are commonly as distinguishable from each other as a Tree from a Hill, or the latter from a Lake; although Clouds in the same modification, considered with respect to each other, have often only the common resemblances which exist among trees, hills, or lakes, taken generally. (…) There are three simple and distinct Modifications, in any one of which the aggregate of minute drops called a Cloud may be formed, increase to its greatest extent and finally decrease and disappear…

68.

AIR.   Always beware of drafts. The depths of the air are invariably unlike the surface; when the former are warm the latter are cold, and vice versa.

CANNON-FIRE.   Affects the weather.

COMETS.   Express scorn for our ancestors who dreaded them.

CORNS.   Better than a barometer for indicating a change in the weather.

MOON.   Inspires melancholy.

OLD MEN.   After a flood or a thunderstorm, or anything of the sort, the old men in the village always say they cannot remember the like of it.

SUMMER.   Always exceptional. (see *Winter*).

WEATHER.   Eternal topic of conversation. Cause of all illnesses. Must always be complained of.

WINTER.   Always exceptional. (see *Summer*).

69.

(Seven Signs of the Plague)

The firste is whan in a sommers day the weder oftentimes chaungeth – as in the morning when the weder appereth to rayn, afterward it aperyth clowdy, and at the last windy in the sowth.

The second token is when in somer the day apperyth all derke and like to rayn, and yet it rayneth not – and if many days so continue, it is to drede of greate pestylence.

The iii token is whan grette multitude of flyes ben upone the erthe – thenne it is a signe that the ayer is venemous and infecte.

The iv token is whan the sterres semen oftetymes to fall – than it is token that the ayer is infecte with moche venomous vapours.

The v token is when a blazyng sterre is sene in the element – then it is signe to be sone aftyr grete pestilence or grete manslagthter in batayle.

The vi token is when ther is grete lightning and thunder, namely owte of the sowthe.

The vii token is when grete windys passyn owte of the sowthe: they ben fowle and onclene. Therfor when these tokenes appere, it is to dred gret pestelence but (unless) God of his gret mercy will remeve it.

70.

I propose to bring to your notice a series of cloud phenomena, which, so far as I can weigh existing evidence, are peculiar to our own times; yet which have not hitherto received any special notice or description from meteorologists. There is no description of it, so far as I have read, or by any ancient observer ... No such clouds as these are, and are now often for months without intermission, were ever seen in the skies of England, France or Italy.

Entering on my immediate subject, I shall best introduce it to you by reading an entry in my diary which gives progressive description of the modern plague-cloud:

> Bolton Abbey, 4th July, 1875. Half-past eight, morning; the first bright morning for the last fortnight. But, an hour ago, the leaves at my window first shook slightly. They are now trembling continuously, as those of all the trees, under a gradually rising wind, of which the tremulous action scarcely permits the direction to be defined – but which falls and returns in fits of varying force, like those which precede a thunderstorm – never wholly ceasing ...

This wind is the plague-wind of the eighth decade of the nineteenth century; a period which will assuredly be recognized in future meteorological history as one of phenomena hitherto unrecorded in the courses of nature, and characterized preeminently by the almost ceaseless action of this calamitous wind. I first noticed the definite character of this wind, and of the clouds it brings with it, in the year 1871, describing it then in the July number of *Fors Clavigera*:

> The first time I recognized the clouds brought by the plague-wind as distinct in character was in walking back from Oxford, after a hard day's work, to Abingdon, in the early spring of 1871 ... And everywhere the leaves of the trees are shaking fitfully, as they do before a thunderstorm; only not violently, but enough to show the passing to and fro of a strange, bitter, blighting wind.

> It looks partly as if it were made of poisonous smoke; very possibly it may be: there are at least two hundred furnace

chimneys in a square of two miles on every side of me. But mere smoke would not blow to and fro in that wild way. It looks more to me as if it were made of dead men's souls—such of them as are not gone yet where they have to go, and may be flitting hither and thither, doubting, themselves, of the fittest place for them.

The last sentence refers of course to the battles of the Franco-German campaign, which was especially horrible to me, in its digging, as the Germans should have known, a moat flooded with waters of death between the two nations for a century to come. Since that Midsummer day, my attention, however otherwise occupied, has never relaxed in its record of the phenomena characteristic of the plague-wind; and I now define for you, as briefly as possible, the essential signs of it.

(1)   It is a wind of darkness – all the former conditions of tormenting winds, whether from the north or east, were more or less capable of coexisting with sunlight; but whenever, and wherever the plague-wind blows, be it but for ten minutes, the sky is darkened instantly.

(2)   It is a malignant quality of wind, unconnected with any one quarter of the compass; it blows indifferently from all, attaching its own bitterness and malice to the worst characters of the proper winds of each quarter.

(3)   It always blows tremulously, making the leaves of the trees shudder as if they were all aspens, but with a peculiar fitfulness which gives them—and I watch them this moment as I write—an expression of anger as well as of fear and distress. You may see the kind of quivering, and hear the ominous whimpering, in the gusts that precede a great thunderstorm; but plague-wind is more panic-struck, and feverish; and its sound is a hiss instead of a wail.

(4)   Not only tremulous at every moment, it is also intermittent with a *rapidity* quite unexampled in former weather ... the light being never for two seconds the same from morning till evening.

Now then – take the following description of thunderstorm *with* plague-wind.

> Brantwood, 13th August, 1879. The most terrific and horrible thunderstorm, this morning, I ever remember. It waked me at six, or a little before—then rolling incessantly, like railway luggage trains, quite ghastly in its mockery of them—the air one loathsome mass of sultry and foul fog, like smoke; scarcely raining at all, but increasing to heavier rollings, with flashes quivering vaguely through all the air, and at last terrific double streams of reddish-violet fire, not forked or zigzag, but rippled rivulets—two at the same instant some twenty to thirty degrees apart, and lasting on the eye at least half a second, with grand artillery-peals following; not rattling crashes, or irregular cracklings, but delivered volleys. It lasted an hour, then passed off, clearing a little, without rain to speak of,—not a glimpse of blue,—and now, half-past seven, seems settling down again into Manchester devil's darkness.

And now I come to the most important sign of the plague-wind and the plague-cloud: that in bringing on their peculiar darkness, they blanch the sun instead of reddening it… In healthy weather, the sun is hidden behind a cloud, as behind a tree; and, when the cloud is past, it comes out again, as bright as before. But in plague-wind, the sun is choked out of the whole heaven, all day long, by a cloud which may be a thousand miles square and five miles deep. (…)

And yet observe: that thin, scraggy, filthy, mangy, miserable cloud, for all the depth of it, can't turn the sun red, as a good, business-like fog does with a hundred feet or so of itself. By the plague-wind every breath of air you draw is polluted, half round the world; in a London fog at least the air itself is pure, though you choose to mix up dirt with it, and choke yourself with your own nastiness…

I should have liked to have sketched for you a bit of plague-cloud to put beside this; but Heaven knows, you can see enough of it nowadays without any trouble of mine; and if you want, in a hurry, to see what the sun looks like through it, you've only to throw a bad half-crown into a basin of soap and water. Blanched Sun – blighted grass – blinded man. If, in conclusion, you ask me for any conceivable cause or meaning of these things – I can tell you none, according to your modern beliefs; but I can tell you what meaning it would have borne to the men of old time. Remember, for the last twenty years, England, and all foreign nations, either tempting her, or following her, have blasphemed the name of God deliberately and openly; and have done iniquity by proclamation, every man doing as much injustice to his brother as it is in his power to do... The Empire of England, on which formerly the sun never set, has become one on which he never rises.

71.

And wene not, for I clepe it a derknes or a cloude, that it be any cloude congelid of the humours that fleen in the ayre, ne yit any derknes soche as is in thine house on nights, when thy candel is oute. For soche a derknes and soche a cloude maist thou ymagin with curiousite of witte, for to bene before thin ighen in the lightest dey of somer; and also, agenswarde, in the derkest night of winter thou mayst ymagin a clere schinyng light. Lat be soche falseheed; I mene not thus. For when I sey derknes, I mene a lackynge of knowing; as alle that thing that thou knowest not, or ells that thou hast forgettyn, it is derk to thee, for thou seest it not with thy goostly ighe. And for this skile it is not clepid a cloude of the eire, bot a cloude of unknowynge, that is betwine thee and thi God.

72.

The second knowledge I have retained from my first ascent is of the inside of a cloud. For, from a few yards above Loch Etchachan to the summit, we walked in a cloud so thick that when the man who was leading went ahead by so much as an arm's length, he vanished, except for his whistle. His wife and I followed the whistle, and now and then when we were too slow (for he was an impatient lad), he materialised again out of the cloud and spoke to us. And alone in that whiteness, while our *revenant* came and went, we climbed an endless way. Nothing altered. Once, our ghostly mentor held us each firmly by an arm and said, 'That's Loch Etchachan down there'. Nothing. The whiteness was perhaps thicker. It was horrible to stand and stare into that pot of whiteness. The path went on. And now to the side of us

there was a ghastlier white, spreading and swallowing even the
grey-brown earth our minds had stood on. We had come to the snow.
A white as of non-life.

73.

Cloud-puffball, torn tufts, tossed pillows flaunt forth, then
       chevy on an air-
built thoroughfare: heaven-roysterers, in gay-gangs they
       throng; they glitter in marches.
Down roughcast, down dazzling whitewash, wherever an elm
       arches,
Shivelights and shadowtackle ín long lashes lace, lance, and
       pair.
Delightfully the bright wind boisterous ropes, wrestles, beats
       earth bare
Of yestertempest's creases; in pool and rutpeel parches
Squandering ooze to squeezed dough, crust, dust; stanches,
       starches
Squadroned masks and manmarks treadmire toil there
Footfretted in it. Million-fuelèd, nature's bonfire burns on.
But quench her bonniest, dearest to her, her clearest-selvèd
       spark
Man, how fast his firedint, his mark on mind, is gone!
Both are in an unfathomable, all is in an enormous dark
Drowned. O pity and indignation! Manshape, that shone
Sheer off, disseveral, a star, death blots black out; nor mark
       Is any of him at all so stark
But vastness blurs and time beats level. Enough! the
       Resurrection,
A heart's-clarion! Away grief's gasping, joyless days, dejection.
       Across my foundering deck shone
A beacon, an eternal beam. Flesh fade, and mortal trash
Fall to the residuary worm; world's wildfire, leave but ash:
       In a flash, at a trumpet crash,
I am all at once what Christ is, since he was what I am, and
This Jack, joke, poor potsherd, patch, matchwood, immortal
       diamond,
       Is immortal diamond.

74.

(*Upon the sight of some variously-coloured clouds*)

There is amongst us a sort of vain and flaunting grandees, who, for their own unhappiness and the age's, do but too much resemble these painted clouds; for both the one and the other are elevated to a station that makes most men look upon them as far above them; and their conspicuousness is often increased by the bright sunshine of the prince's favour, which, though it really leaves them creatures of the same frail nature that it found them, does yet give them a lustre and a gaudiness, that much attracts the eyes, and perhaps the envy and respect of those superficial gazers upon things, that are wont to be amused, if not dazzled, with their insignificant outsides.

But the parallel holds further; for as, in spite of these clouds' sublimity and conspicuousness, they are but airy and unsolid things, consisting of vapours, and steered by every wind; so the fine people I am comparing them to, in spite of their exaltation, and of all the show they make, are really but slight persons, destitute of intrinsic and solid worth, and guided either by their own blind lusts and passions, or else by interests as fickle as those, to which it will be no addition to say, or/ are as variable as the wind. And as these clouds, though they seem vast as well as high, and are, perhaps, able for a while to make the sky somewhat dark, have usually but a short duration, and either quickly fall down in rain, or are quite dissipated and made to disappear; so these titled persons... and this ruin sometimes happens to the most elevated persons, from that very prince, whose favour made them attract so many eyes; as clouds are oftentimes dispersed before night by the same sun that had raised and gilded them in the morning.

75.

Come, ascend the ladder: all come in: all sit down.
We were poor, poor, poor, poor, poor,
When we came to this world through the poor place,
Where the body of water dried for our passing.
Banked up clouds cover the earth.
All come four times with your showers:

Descend to the base of the ladder & stand still:
Bring your showers & great rains.
All, all come, all ascend, all come in, all sit down.

> (*the stanza is repeated four times*)

76.

In Kursk, a province of Southern Russia, when rain is much wanted, the women seize a passing stranger and throw him into the river, or souse him from head to foot. Later on we shall see that a passing stranger is often taken for a deity or the personification of some natural power. It is recorded in official documents that during a drought in 1790 the peasants of Scheroutz and Werboutz collected all the women and compelled them to bathe, in order that rain might fall. An Armenian rain-charm is to throw the wife of a priest into the water and drench her. The Arabs of North Africa fling a holy man, willy-nilly, into a spring as a remedy for drought. In Minahassa, a province of North Celebes, the priest bathes as a rain-charm. In Central Celebes when there has been no rain for a long time and the rice-stalks begin to shrivel up, many of the villagers, especially the young folk, go to a neighbouring brook and splash each other with water, shouting noisily, or squirt water on one another through bamboo tubes. Sometimes they imitate the plump of rain by smacking the surface of the water with their hands, or by placing an inverted gourd on it and drumming on the gourd with their fingers.

77.

A sieve of rain lengthens thickens
over house over field over forest

same view
as in 1967
only in the place
where lupines grew
rye fades in color

closely spaced raindrops
peck away at the tin windowsill
the same view
only without the white
shepherd dog
Bari was killed
and skinned
his doghouse was dismantled
its place overgrown by grass

and he was such a faithful dog
so obedient
he loved to eat and was so thankful
for every bite
every scrap

and he really knew how to be happy
how to greet you how to look you in the eye

78.

I am in the third circle of eternal, malicious rain, cold and weighted
rain whose rhythm and kind never change;

heavy hail, dirty water and snow pour down through the shadowy air,
the ground stinks where it lands.

Cerberus, savage and odd, barks dog-threats through three throats
over the people sunk there.

He has red eyes, his beard is greasy and black, his belly huge, his
hands clawed; he scratches the spirits, shreds and dismembers them.

The rain makes them howl like dogs: they use one side of their body
to shelter the other side, poor sinners, turning this way and that.

When he saw us, Cerberus that vast worm, opened his mouths and
showed his fangs; not one of his limbs not moving.

My guide spread his hands and took some soil and with both fists
full, threw it inside those eager jaws.

Like a dog that yelps for food and goes quiet while it chews, putting
all its attention into eating,

that's how his horrible faces looked, which had been bellowing at the
souls until they longed for deafness.

We walked over the rain-flattened shadows, putting our feet down on
a nothingness that always seemed to be someone.

They were lying there on the ground, all but one who sat up as soon
as he saw us pass.

'Whoever you are being dragged through this Hell' he said,
'remember me if you can: you were being made before I was unmade.'

I said to him: 'your anguish has perhaps cancelled you from my
memory, so that I can't recall ever having seen you.

But tell me who you are, caught in such a sad place; perhaps there are
greater punishments than yours but none so disgusting.'

He said to me: 'Your city, so full of envy that the sack is bursting, gave
me a good life.

Your people called me Ciacco. For my punishable gluttony I have to
lie here as you see me helpless in the rain.

I am not the only sad spirit, all these face the same punishment for
the same fault.' That's all he said.

79.

Careful Observers may foretel the Hour
(By sure Prognosticks) when to dread a Show'r:
While Rain depends, the pensive Cat gives o'er

Her Frolicks, and pursues her Tail no more.
Returning Home at Night, you'll find the Sink
Strike your offended Sense with double Stink.
If you be wise, then go not far to Dine,
You'll spend in Coach-hire more than save in Wine.
A coming Show'r your shooting Corns presage,
Old Aches throb, your hollow Tooth will rage.
Sauntering in Coffeehouse is *Dulman* seen;
He damns the Climate, and complains of Spleen.

Meanwhile the South, rising with dabbled Wings,
A Sable Cloud athwart the Welkin flings,
That swill'd more Liquor than it could contain,
And like a Drunkard gives it up again.
Brisk *Susan* whips her Linen from the Rope,
While the first drizzling Show'r is born aslope:
Such is that Sprinkling which some careless Quean
Flirts on you from her Mop, but not so clean.
You fly, invoke the Gods; then turning, stop
To rail; she singing, still whirls on her Mop.
Not yet, the dust had shunn'd th'unequal Strife,
But, aided by the Wind, fought still for Life,
And wafted with its Foe by violent Gust,
'Twas doubtful which was Rain, and which was Dust.
Ah! where must needy Poet seek for Aid,
When Dust and Rain at once his Coat invade?
Sole Coat, where Dust cemented by the Rain,
Erects the Nap, and leaves a cloudy Stain.

Now in contiguous Drops the Flood comes down,
Threat'ning with Deluge this *Devoted* Town.
To shops in Crowds the daggled Females fly,
Pretend to cheapen Goods, but nothing buy.
The Templar spruce, while every Spout's a-broach,
Stays till 'tis fair, yet seems to call a Coach.
The tuck'd-up Sempstress walks with hasty Strides,
While seams run down her oil'd Umbrella's Sides.
Here various Kinds, by various Fortunes led,

Commence Acquaintance underneath a Shed.
Triumphant Tories and desponding Whigs
Forget their Feuds, and join to save their Wigs.
Box'd in a chair the Beau impatient sits,
While Spouts run clattering o'er the Roof by Fits;
And ever and anon with frightful Din
The Leather sounds; he trembles from within.
So when Troy Chair-men bore the Wooden Steed,
Pregnant with *Greeks*, impatient to be freed,
(Those bully *Greeks*, who, as the Moderns do,
Instead of paying Chair-men, run them through),
Laocoön struck the Outside with his Spear,
And each imprison'd hero quak'd for Fear.

Now from all Parts the swelling Kennels flow,
And bear their Trophies with them as they go:
Filth of all Hues and Odours seem to tell
What Streets they sailed from, by their Sight and Smell.
They, as each Torrent drives, with rapid Force
From *Smithfield* or St. *Pulchre's* shape their Course,
And in huge Confluence join at *Snow-Hill* Ridge,
Fall from the *Conduit* prone to *Holborn Bridge*.
Sweepings from Butchers' Stalls, Dung, Guts, and Blood,
Drown'd Puppies, stinking Sprats, all drench'd in Mud,
Dead Cats and Turnip-tops come tumbling down the Flood.

80.

Sun 29 May 1825. Heard the most severe thunderclap yesterday that I
ever heard in my life it was heard instantly (only 3 pulses) after the
flash — Found a very scarce & curious orchis of an iron grey color or
rather a pale rusty tinge with a root like the pilewort I cannot make
out its name — I found last week a fine white pigeon orchis which is
seldom found. Mon 30 May 1825. Took a walk yesterday to Bassetts
close at the bottom of the wormstalls to see the Ash tree that the
lightning struck on Saturday it took off the large top & splinterd
the body to atoms driving large pieces of it in all directions round the
tree to the distance of fifty yards the stump of the trunk left standing

was pilled of the bark all round & split to the bottom. I never saw
such terrible power of lightning in my life before: people came to see
it from all the neighbouring villages & took away the fragments as
curiositys

81.

The tall transformer stood
Biblically glorified, and then turned blue.
Space split. The earth tossed twelve hens in the air.
The landscape's hair stood up. The collie flew,
Or near it, back to the house and vanished there.

Roofed by a gravel pit,
I, in a safe place, as I always am,
Was, as I always am, observer only
– Nor cared. Why should I? The belief's a sham
That shared danger or escape cures being lonely.

Yet when I reached the croft
They excluded me by telling me. As they talked
Across my failure, I turned away to see
Hills spouting white and a huge cloud that walked
With a million million legs on to the sea.

82.

Salmoneus lived at first in Thessaly, but afterwards he came to Elis
and there founded a city. A man of great arrogance, he wished to put
himself on an equality with Zeus, and was punished for his impiety.
For he claimed that he himself was Zeus, and depriving the god of his
sacrifices, he ordered them to be offered up to himself instead. And
by dragging dried animal hides and bronze kettles behind his chariot,
he said that he was making thunder; and by flinging lighted torches
into the sky he said that he was making lightning. But Zeus struck
him down with a thunderbolt, and wiped out the city he had
founded, with all its inhabitants.

83.

The market is a huge roofed-in place. Most extraordinary is the noise that comes out, as you pass along the adjacent street. It is a huge noise, yet you may never notice it. It sounds as if all the ghosts in the world were talking to one another, in ghost-voices, within the darkness of the market structure. It is a noise something like rain, or banana leaves in a wind. The market, full of Indians, dark-faced, silent-footed, hush-spoken, but pressing in in countless numbers. The queer hissing murmurs of the Zapotec *idioma*, among the sounds of Spanish, the quiet, aside-voices of the Mixtecas…

84.

To Mr. Henry White, a young clergyman, with whom he now formed an intimacy, so as to talk to him with great freedom, he mentioned that he could not in general accuse himself of having been an undutiful son. 'Once, indeed (said he), I was disobedient; I refused to attend my father to Uttoxeter market. Pride was the source of that refusal, and the remembrance of it was painful. A few years ago, I desired to atone for this fault: I went to Uttoxeter in very bad weather, and stood for a considerable time bare-headed in the rain, on the spot where my father's stall used to stand. In contrition I stood, and I hope the penance was expiatory.'

85.

Like in Autumn when the blind earth is flattened by winds and Zeus drops down his heaviest rains enraged with men for thinking they can't be seen

in their rough law-courts with their crooked judgements with their scorn of Justice

when the rivers burst their banks and runnels gouge into hillsides and it howls all the way from the summit to the blackened sea

washing all our industry to nothing (that was the noise of the earth when those horses were running …)

86.

The tamarack can cut rain down to size, mist-little
bead-gauze, hold at needlepoint a plenty
and from the going, blue-sunk storm keep a

shadow, glittery recollection: the heart-leaved
big hydrangea bends over blossom-nodding, a few
large drops and a general glaze streaking leaves

with surface tension: the maple leaves
gather hail-size drops at the lobes and
sway them ragged loose: spirea, quince, cedar,

elm, hollyhock, clover (a sharp header)
permit various styles of memory: then the sun
breaks out and clears the record of what is gone.

87.

Greta Hall, Keswick. My dear Sir, the River is full, and Lodore is full,
and silver Fillets come out of Clouds, & glitter in every Ravine of all
the mountains, and the Hail lies, like Snow, upon their Tops, & the
impetuous Gusts from Borrodale snatch the water up high &
continually at the bottom of the Lake; it is not distinguishable from
Snow slanting before the wind — and under this seeming Snow-drift
the Sunshine *gleams*, & over all the hither Half of the Lake it is
bright, and dazzles — a cauldron of melted Silver boiling! It is in very
truth a sunny, misty, cloudy, dazzling, howling, omniform, Day.

88.

              .. And so I long for snow to
sweep across the low heights of London
from the lonely railyards and trackhuts
– London a lichen mapped on mild clays
and its rough circle without purpose –
because I remember the gap for clarity

that comes before snow in the north and
I remember the lucid air's changing sky
and I remember the grey-black wall with
every colour imminent in a coming white
the moon rising only to be displaced and
the measured volatile calmness of after
and I remember the blue snow hummocks
the mountains of miles off in snow-light
frozen lakes – a frozen moss to stand on
where once a swarmed drifting stopped.
And I think – we need such a change,
my city and I, that may be conjured in
us that dream birth of compassion with
reason and energy merged in slow dance.

89.

No talking, no talking.
The snow is falling.
And the wind seems to be blowing backward.

90.

Wishing to offer my benefactor, Counsellor Wacker, who is a devotee
of Nothing, a gift which shall itself be practically nothing … It must
be both exiguous and diminutive, inexpensive and ephemeral. One of
Epicurus's atoms would not do, for that would be simply nothing at
all. The Elements likewise – Earth, Fire, Air, and Water – are reviewed
in turn, but rejected as unsuitable…

With such anxious reflections as these I crossed the Charles
Bridge, embarrassed by my discourtesy in appearing before you
without a New Year's gift, except insofar as I harp ceaselessly on the
same chord and repeatedly bring forth Nothing: vexed too at not
finding what is next to nothing, yet lends itself to sharpness of wit.
Just then, by a happy chance, water-vapour was being condensed by
cold into snow, some flakes of which fell here and there on my coat –
all of them with six corners and feathered radii. Upon my word! Here

was something smaller than any droplet, yet with a pattern; here was the ideal New Year's gift for the connoisseur of Nothing, the very thing for a mathematician to give, who has nothing and receives nothing – since it comes down from heaven and looks like a star (…)

Our question is: why do snowflakes in their first falling always have six corners and six rods tufted like feathers? I looked to the Psalmist, who records among the praises of God that 'He giveth snow like wool', and who probably observed these little stars of snow settling on the fleeces of his sheep (…)

But as quickly as my snowflake melts I rebut my own trivial reasonings with counter-instances, and reduce them all to – nothing.

91.

Basho, coming
To the city of Nagoya,
Is asked to a snow party.

There is a tinkling of china
And tea into china;
There are introductions.

Then everyone
Crowds to the window
To watch the falling snow.

Snow is falling on Nagoya
And farther south
On the tiles of Kyoto;

Eastward, beyond Irago,
It is falling
Like leaves on the cold sea.

Elsewhere they are burning
Witches and heretics
In the boiling squares,

Thousands have died since dawn
In the service
Of barbarous kings;

But there is silence
In the houses of Nagoya
And the hills of Ise.

92.

One day, when the snow lay thick on the ground and it was so cold
that the lattices had all been closed, I and the other ladies were sitting
with Her Majesty, chatting and poking the embers in the brazier.

'Tell me, Shonagon,' said the Empress, 'how is the snow on
Hsiang-lu peak?'

I told the maid to raise one of the lattices and then rolled up the
blind all the way. Her Majesty smiled. I was not alone in recognizing
the Chinese poem she had quoted; in fact all the ladies knew the lines
and had even rewritten them in Japanese. Yet no one but me had
managed to think of it instantly.

'Yes, indeed,' people said when they heard the story. 'She was born
to serve an Empress like ours.'

93.

The room was suddenly rich and the great bay-window was
Spawning snow and pink roses against it
Soundlessly collateral and incompatible:
World is suddener than we fancy it.

World is crazier and more of it than we think,
Incorrigibly plural. I peel and portion
A tangerine and spit the pips and feel
The drunkenness of things being various.

And the fire flames with a bubbling sound for world
Is more spiteful and gay than one supposes –
On the tongue on the eyes on the ears in the palms of one's hands –
There is more than glass between the snow and the huge roses.

94.

Snow gives a singular colour to the entire universe which, with that one word 'snow', is both expressed and nullified for those who have found shelter. Outside the house, the winter cosmos is a simplified cosmos. It is a non-house in the same way that metaphysicians speak of a non-I, and between the house and the non-house it is easy to establish all sorts of contradictions. Inside the house, everything may be differentiated and multiplied. The house derives reserves and refinements of intimacy from winter; while in the outside world, snow covers all tracks, blurs the road, muffles every sound, conceals all colours. As a result of this universal whiteness, we feel a form of cosmic negation in action. The dreamer of houses knows and senses this, and because of the diminished entity of the outside world, experiences all the qualities of intimacy with increased intensity.

Winter is by far the oldest of the seasons. Not only does it confer age upon our memories, taking us back to a remote past but, on snowy days, the house too is old. It is as though it were living in the past of centuries gone by.

An immense cosmic house is the potential of every dream of houses. Winds radiate from its centre and gulls fly from its windows.

95.

First snow is never all the snows there were
Come back again, but novel in the sun
As though a newness had but just begun.

It does not fall as rain does from nowhere
Or from that cloud spinnakered on the blue,
But from a place we feel we could go to.

As a great actor steps, not from the wings,
But from the play's extension – all he does
Is move to the seen from the mysterious –

And his performance is the first of all –
The snow falls from its implications and
Stages pure newness on the uncurtained land.

And the hill we've looked out of existence comes
Vivid in its own language; and this tree
Stands self-explained, its own soliloquy.

96.

One morning after a pleasant fall of snow I sent a letter to someone
with whom I had business, but failed to mention the snow. The reply
was droll: 'Do you suppose I can pay any attention to someone so
perverse as to write a letter with no word of inquiry about how I am
enjoying the snow? I am most disappointed in you.' Now that the
author of that letter is dead, even so trivial an incident sticks in my
mind.

97.

28 Jan 1787. I read Prayers and Preached this morning at Weston
Church neither Mr. or Mrs. Custance at Church, nor above 20
People in all at Church – The Weather being extremely cold and
severe with much Snow on the ground and still more falling with
cutting Winds. After Service I buried a Daughter of Harrisons an
Infant aged only 5 Weeks – I think that I never felt the cold more
severe than when I was burying the above Infant. The Wind blowed
very Strong and Snow falling all the time and the Wind almost
directly in my Face, that it almost stopped my breath in reading the
funeral Service at the Grave, tho' I had an Umbrella I held over my
Head during the Time.

98.

The seductive folds of the sleeping bag.
The hiss of the primus and the fragrant steam of the cooker
issuing from the tent ventilator.

The small green tent and the great white road.
The whine of a dog and the neigh of our steeds.
The driving cloud of powdered snow.
The crunch of footsteps which break the surface crust.
The wind-blown furrows.
The blue arch beneath the smoky cloud.
The crisp ring of the ponies' hooves and the ring of the following
sledge.
The droning conversation of the march as driver encourages or
chides his horse.
The patter of dog pads.
The gentle flutter of our canvas shelter.
Its deep booming sound under the full force of a blizzard.
The drift snow like finest flour penetrating every hole and corner
– flickering up beneath one's head covering, pricking
sharply as a sand blast.
The sun with blurred image peeping shyly through the
wreathing drift giving pale shadowless light.
The eternal silence of the great white desert. Cloudy columns of
snow drift advancing from the south, pale yellow wraiths,
heralding the coming storm, blotting out one by one the
sharp-cut lines of the land ...

99.

And as in winter time when Jove his cold-sharpe javelines throwes
Amongst us mortals and is mov'd to white earth with his snowes
(The winds asleepe) he freely poures, till highest Prominents,
Hill tops, low meddowes and the fields that crowne with most
    contents
The toiles of men, sea ports and shores are hid, and everie place
But floods (that snowe's faire tender flakes, as their own brood,
    embrace):
So both sides cover'd earth with stones, so both for life contend
To shew their sharpnesse.

100.

And an old man, Antenor, who was by us said, 'That indeed is
Odysseus. I remember that he and Menelaus came on an embassy to
the assembly of the Trojans. When they both stood up, Menelaus
seemed the greater man, but when they sat down Odysseus seemed
the more stately. When he spoke with cunning in the assembly,
Menelaus was rapid and skilful of speech. When Odysseus got to his
feet, he just stood there with his eyes fixed to the ground, making no
movement with his staff either backwards or forwards, but gripping
it like an idiot. You'd think he was completely witless, but when he
spoke the words flew about our ears like a storm of snowflakes, his
great voice resonated, and then no mortal could contend with him.'

101.

When the Ice is fixed upon the Sea, you see a snow-white
brightness in the Skies, as if the Sun shined, for the Snow is
reflected by the Air, just as a Fire by Night is; but at a distance you
see the Air blew or blackish: where there is many small Ice-fields,
that are as the Meadows for the *Seales*, you see no lustre or
brightness of the Skies. The Sea dasheth against these Ice-fields,
which occasioneth several fine Figures; not that they are naturally
framed so, but just as Ice flowers on our Glas-windows get all sorts
of figures; for these are framed by the dashing of the Sea like unto
Mountains, Steeples, Tables, Chappels, and all sorts of Beasts ...
The highest colour is delicate Blew, of the same colour with the
Blewest Vitriol.

102.

When we were at sea, junketting, tippling, discoursing, and telling
Stories, *Pantagruel* rose and stood up to look out; then ask'd us, 'Do
you hear nothing, Gentlemen? Methinks I hear some People talking
in the Air, yet I can see no Body. Hark!' According to his command

we listened, and with full ears suck'd in the Air, as some of you suck Oysters, to find if we could hear some Sound scatter'd through the Sky; and to lose none of it, like the Emperor *Antoninus* some of us laid their Hands hollow next to their Ears; but all this would not do, nor could we hear any Voice. Yet *Pantagruel* continued to assure us he heard various Voices in the Air, some of Men, and some of Women.

At last we began to fancy that we also heard something, or at least, that our Ears tingled; and the more we listen'd, the plainer we discern'd the Voices, so as to distinguish articulate Sounds. This mightily frighten'd us, and not without Cause, since we could see nothing, yet heard such various Sounds and Voices of Men, Women, Children, Horses, &c., insomuch that *Panurge* cry'd out, 'Cods-Belly, there is no fooling with the Devil; we are all beshit, let's fly. There is some Ambuscado hereabouts.' (…)

The skipper made answer: 'Be not afraid, my lord, we are on the Confines of the Frozen Sea, on which, about the Beginning of last Winter, happen'd a great and bloody Fight between the *Arimaspians* and the *Nephelibates*. Then the Words and Cries of Men and Women, the hacking, slashing, and hewing of Battle-axes, the shocking, knocking, and jolting of Armours, and Harnesses, the neighing of horses, and all other martial Din and Noise, froze in the Air; and now the Rigour of the winter being over, by the succeeding Serenity and Warmth of the Weather, they melt and are heard.'

'By Jingo,' quoth *Panurge*, 'the Man talks somewhat like. I believe him. But couldn't we see some of 'em? I think I have read, that on the Edge of the Mountain on which *Moses* receiv'd the *Judaic* law, the People saw the Voices sensibly.' – 'Here, here,' said *Pantagruel*, 'here are some that are not yet thaw'd.' He then throw'd us on the Deck whole Handfuls of frozen Words, which seem'd to us like your rough Sugar-Plums, of many Colours, like those us'd in Heraldry; some words *Gules* (this means also Jests and merry Sayings), some *Vert*, some *Azur*, some *Black*, some *Or* (this means fine fair Words); and when we had somewhat warm'd them between our Hands, they melted like Snow, and we really heard them, but could not understand them, for it was a barbarous Gibberish. One of them only, that was pretty big, having been warm'd between Friar *John's* Hands, gave a Sound much like that of Chestnuts when they are thrown into the Fire without being first cut, which made us all start. 'This was the report of a Field-piece in its time,' cry'd Fryar *John*.

Panurge pray'd *Pantagruel* to give him some more; but *Pantagruel* told him, that to give Words was the Part of a Lover. 'Sell me some then, I pray you,' cry'd Panurge. 'That's the part of a lawyer,' returned *Pantagruel*. 'I would sooner sell you Silence, tho' at a dearer Rate.'

However, he threw three or four Handfuls of them on the Deck; among which I perceiv'd some very sharp Words, and some bloody Words, which the pilot said, us'd sometime to go back and recoil to the Place whence they came, but it was with a slit Weasand; we also saw some terrible Words, and some others not very pleasant to the Eye.

When they had been all melted together, we heard a strange Noise, hin, hin, hin, hin, his, tick, tock, taack, brededin, brededack, frr, frr, frr, bou, bou, bou, bou, bou, bou, bou, bou, track, track, trr, trr, trr, trrr, trrrrrr, on, on, on, on, on, on, ouououon, gog, magog, and I do not know what other barbarous Words, which the pilot said were the Noise made by the charging Squadrons, the Shock and Neighing of Horses.

Then we heard some large ones go off like Drums and Fifes, and others like Clarions and Trumpets. Believe me, we had very good Sport with them. I would fain have sav'd some merry odd Words, and have preserv'd them in Oil, as Ice and Snow are kept, and between clean Straw. But *Pantagruel* would not let me, saying that 'tis a Folly to hoard up what we are never like to want, or have always at Hand: odd, quaint, merry, and fat Words of *Gules* never being scarce among all good and jovial *Pantagruelists*.

103.

May I, for my own self, song's truth reckon,
Journey's jargon, how I in harsh days
Hardship endured oft.
Bitter breast-cares have I abided,
Known on my keel many a care's hold,
And dire sea-surge, and there I oft spent
Narrow nightwatch nigh the ship's head
While she tossed close to cliffs. Coldly afflicted,
My feet were by frost benumbed.
Chill its chains are; chafing sighs

Hew my heart round and hunger begot
Mere-weary mood. Lest man know not
That he on dry land loveliest liveth,
List how I, care-wretched, on ice-cold sea,
Weathered the winter, wretched outcast
Deprived of my kinsmen;
Hung with hard ice-flakes, where hail-scur flew,
There I heard naught save the harsh sea
And ice-cold wave, at whiles the swan cries,
Did for my games the gannet's clamour,
Sea-fowls' loudness was for me laughter,
The mews' singing all my mead-drink.
Storms, on the stone-cliffs beaten, fell on the stern
In icy feathers; full oft the eagle screamed
With spray on his pinion.

104.

'So I, careworn, deprived of fatherland,
Far from my noble kin, have often had
To tie in fetters my own troubled spirit,
Since long ago I wrapped my lord's remains
In darkness of the earth, and sadly thence
Journeyed by winter over icy waves,
And, suffering, sought the hall of a new patron,
If I in any land might find one willing
To show me recognition in his mead-hall,
Comfort my loneliness, tempt me with warmth (…)

But then the friendless man wakes again
And sees instead the yellow waves,
The sea-birds bathing, stretching their feathers,
While snow and hail and frost fall all together.

                    Care is renewed
For one who must continually send
His weary spirit over icy waves (…)

The wise man must know how fearful it will be
When all the wealth of the earth stands desolate,
As now in various parts throughout the world
Stand wind-blown walls, frost-covered, ruined homes.
The wine-halls crumble; monarchs lifeless lie,
Deprived of pleasures, all the company of heroes
Dead by the wall (…)

And storms now beat against these stony slopes.
Falling sleet and snow fetter the world
In winter's vice; then darkness comes and
Shadowy night approaches; the north sends down
Fierce hailstorms in malice against men.
And all is hardship in this earthly kingdom; the work
Of fate alters the world lying beneath the heavens.
Here belongings and friends pass away;
Here man and kinsman pass away;
And all this earthly structure is a wilderness.'
Thus spoke the thoughtful sage, as he sat apart, meditating.

105.

If anyone *there* still remembers exiled Ovid, if my
      name survives in the City now I'm gone,
let him know that beneath those stars that never dip in Ocean
      I live now in mid-Barbary, hemmed about
by wild Sarmatians, Bessi, Getae, names unworthy
      of my talent! Yet so long as the warm breezes
still blow, the Danube between defends us:
      its flowing waters keep off all attacks.
But when grim winter thrusts forth his rough-set visage,
      and earth lies white under marmoreal frost,
when gales and blizzards make the far northern regions
      unfit for habitation, then Danube's ice
feels the weight of those creaking wagons. Snow falls: once fallen
      it lies for ever, wind-frosted. Neither sun
nor rain can shift it. Before one fall's melted, another
      comes, and in many places lies two years,

and so fierce the gales, they wrench off rooftops, whirl them
      headlong, skittle tall towers.
Men keep out this aching cold with furs and stiched breeches,
      only their faces left exposed,
and often the hanging ice in their hair tinkles,
      while beards gleam white with frost.
Wine stands unbottled, retaining the shape of its vessel,
      so that what you get to drink isn't liquor, but lumps.
Shall I describe how the cold here freezes rivers solid,
      how fissile water's chopped from icy ponds
how the very Danube – Nile boasts no broader delta,
      nor more numerous outlets to the deep –
will freeze as the winds stiff-whip its dark-blue waters,
      and winds its way seaward under ice?
Where ships had sailed before, men go on foot now, horses'
      hoofbeats ring out on frozen waves,
and across new bridges, the current gliding under,
      Sarmatian oxen haul rough native carts.
I can hardly hope for credence – yet since a falsehood
      gets no reward, the witness should be credited:
I've seen the wide sea iced solid, a frozen slippery
      crust holding the under-water still –
not just seen, either. I've walked the solid sea-lanes,
      crunching their surface dryfoot. Leander, if you
had had *that* sort of strait to cross, your death would never
      have been a charge on the narrows. At such times
even the arching dolphins cannot launch themselves skyward:
      harsh winter checks their every attempt, and though
the north wind screams aloud, with hurling wingspread,
      no comber will surge up from the hard-
packed flood, hulls ringd with ice will stand fast as in marble,
      no oar will cleave those stiff waves.
(I've seen fish frozen into the ice – yet notwithstanding
      some still survived, and thawed.)
So whether these tearing northers harden up sea-water
      or the brimming river, as soon
as the Danube's been frozen level by their ice-dry wind-chill
      hordes of hostile savages ride over on swift

ponies, their pride, with bows that shoot long-range arrows
　　　and cut a marauding swath throgh the countryside.
Some neighbours flee, and with none to protect their steadings
　　　their property, unguarded, makes quick loot:
mean rustic household goods, flocks and creaking wagons,
　　　all the wealth a poor local peasant has ...

106.

A curious creature came floating over the waves,
shouting her beauty to the distant shores,
resounding loudly; her laughter was terrible,
fearsome to all; and her edges were sharp.
She is slow to join battle but fierce in fray,
smashing great ships with savagery.
She binds them with her baleful charms
and speaks with native cunning:
'My mother, one of the belovèd maidens,
is also my daughter, swollen and strong,
known to all peoples as she courses the earth,
welcomed with love in every land.'   (iceberg)

107.

　　　　　I

Who affirms that crystals are alive?
　　　I affirm it, let who will deny: –
Crystals are engendered, wax and thrive,
　　　Wane and wither: I have seen them die.

Trust me, masters, crystals have their day,
　　　Eager to attain the perfect norm,
Lit with purpose, potent to display
　　　Facet, angle, colour, beauty, form.

II

Water-crystals need for flower and root
    Sixty clear degrees, no less, no more;
Snow, so fickle, still in this acute
    Angle thinks, and learns no other lore:

Such its life, and such its pleasure is,
    Such its art and traffic, such its gain,
Evermore in new conjunctions this
    Admirable angle to maintain.

Crystalcraft in every flower and flake
    Snow exhibits, of the welkin free:
Crystalline are crystals for the sake,
    All and singular, of crystalry.

Yet does every crystal of the snow
    Individualise, a seedling sown
Broadcast, but instinct with power to grow
    Beautiful in beauty of its own.

Every flake with all its prongs and dints
    Burns ecstatic as a new-lit star:
Men are not more diverse, finger prints
    More dissimilar than snow-flakes are.

Worlds of men and snow endure, increase,
    Woven of power and passion to defy
Time and travail: only races cease,
    Individual men and crystals die.

III

Jewelled shapes of snow whose feathery showers,
    Fallen or falling wither at a breath,
All afraid are they, and loth as flowers
    Beasts and men to tread the way to death.

Once I saw upon an object-glass,
      Martyred underneath a microscope,
One elaborate snow-flake slowly pass,
      Dying hard, beyond the reach of hope.

Still from shape to shape the crystal changed,
      Writhing in its agony; and still,
Less and less elaborate, arranged
      Potently the angle of its will.

Tortured to a simple final form,
      Angles six and six divergent beams,
Lo, in death it touched the perfect norm
      Verifying all its crystal dreams!

IV

Such the noble tragedy of one
      Martyred snow-flake. Who can tell the fate
Heinous and uncouth of showers undone,
      Fallen in cities! – showers that expiate

Errant lives from polar worlds adrift
      Where the great millennial snows abide;
Castaways from mountain-chains that lift
      Snowy summits in perennial pride;

Nomad snows, or snows in evil day
      Born to urban ruin, to be tossed,
Trampled, shovelled, ploughed, and swept away
      Down the seething sewers: all the frost

Flowers of heaven melted up with lees,
      Offal, recrement, but every flake
Showing to the last in fixed degrees
      Perfect crystals for the crystal's sake.

V

Usefulness of snow is but a chance
      Here in temperate climes with winter sent,
Sheltering earth's prolonged hibernal trance:
      All utility is accident.

Sixty clear degrees the joyful snow,
      Practising economy of means,
Fashions endless beauty in, and so
      Glorifies the universe with scenes

Arctic and antarctic: stainless shrouds,
      Ermine woven in silvery frost, attire
Peaks in every land among the clouds
      Crowned with snows to catch the morning's fire.

108.

I want to report to you an observation I made during the past winter of 1635. On the fourth of February, the air having previously been extremely cold, there fell in the evening in Amsterdam (where I was at that time) a little frost, which is to say, rain which froze upon striking the earth. And afterwards a very fine hail, whose particles I judged to be drops of the same rain, which were frozen high in the air. Nevertheless, instead of being exactly round, as doubtless these drops had been, they had one side notably flatter than the other, so that they almost resembled in shape the part of our eye called the crystalline humour. From this I understood that the wind, which was then quite strong and very cold, had the necessary force so to change the shape of the drops in freezing them. But what astonished me most of all was that among those grains of hail which fell last, I had noticed some which had six tiny teeth around them, similar to those in the wheels of a clock. And these teeth were very white, like sugar, whereas the grains, which were of transparent ice, seemed to be nearly black...

109.

Albert Szent-Gyorgyi, who knew a thing or two about maps,
       by which life moves somewhere or other,
       used to tell this story from the war,
       through which history moves somewhere or other:

'The young lieutenant of a small Hungarian detachment in the Alps
       sent out a reconnaissance unit into the icy wastes.
       At once
       it began to snow, it snowed for two days and the unit
       did not return. The lieutenant suffered: he had sent
       his own men to their deaths.

But on the third day the unit returned.
       Where had they been? How did they find their way back?
       Yes, they said, we considered ourselves
       lost and waited for the end. Then one of us
       found a map in his pocket. That reassured us.
       We pitched camp, waited for the snow to stop, and then
          with the map
       we found our bearings.
       And here we are.

The lieutenant asked to see this remarkable map
       and had a good look at it. It was not a map of the Alps
       but of the Pyrenees.'

Goodbye.

110.

In Februar come foul days, flee them gin ye may,
wi their felloun frosts, days that wad flype a nowt,
whan Boreas blaws owre Thrace, whaur they breed the horses,
and brulyies the braid sea, and gars it blawp;
and the winterous warld and the woddis warsle aathegither.
Monie a michty aik-tree and muckle-heidit pine

it dings til the dirt, our genetrice; wi the dunt as it faas
on the glens and the gowls atween the hills, syne the hale forest girns.
It garrs the bestiall grue; their tails in the grooves
of their hurdies are steikit weill hame. The hairy yins and aa,
wi coats of guid cleidin, it cuts richt throu them;
the weill-happit hide of an ox, that duisnae haud out the cauld.
And it gangs throu a gait's lang hair. But gimmers and yowes
wi fouth of fleece, the wund flegs them nocht,
tho it bends an auld man's back, bow'd like a wheel.
And it canna skaith the saft skin of a young lass
that bienlie bides at hame, beside her dear mither,
onwittand as yet the ongauns of maist aureat Aphrodite.
But she wesches weill her flesch, and wycelie anoints it
wi ulyie of the best olives, syne beddis ben the hous.
The Baneless Yin bites his fuit, tholan bad weather—
wi nae heat frae hearth-stane, the hous is dowie.
The sun sairs him nocht to seek his food outbye;
he swees owre the cities of swart savage folk
but frae his saitt celestial is sweirt to shine on the Greeks.
Syne the hirsel of hornit kye, and the hornless baists,
wend throu the wuids: wearily they grind their teeth,
thirlit in aefald thocht, to find in their need
a bield to bide in, or a boss cave.
Trauchlit in siccan times, they traivel about
like luttaird loons that limp on three legs
wi lumbago in the lunyie, aye luikan on the grund;
they hirple hobland about, hap-schackellit they seem;
hainan their bodies' heat, haud awa frae the white snaw-wreaths.
Sae pit on, I pray ye, as protection for yir flesch,
a saft goun and a sark streetchan to yir feet;
let it be woven wi muckle weft til a puckle warp,
that the hairs of yir bodie may be at rest, no birssy wi the cauld …
Mak yirsel a kid-skin cape to keep out the rain,
and a felt hat wi laced lappits, syne yir lugs will be dry;
for yir neb will be nithert whan the nor-wund blaws;
at day-daw the hairst-nourissand haar, frae the hevin of sterns,
blankets the braid yird, bieldan the parks of the rich.
The haar soukit in steam frae ever-bounteous stremis
is blawn heich abuin the yird by blaisters of wund.

At dirknin it whiles draws to rain; whiles the blast's deray
is ruggan at thwankan cluddis thruschit by Thracian Boreas.

111.

Lapt up in sacks to shun the rain & wind
& shoes thick clouted with the sticking soil
& sidelings on his horse the careless hind
Rides litherly & singing to his toil
The boy rides foremost where the sack is gone
& holds with his hands to keep it on
Then splashing down the road in journey slow
Through mire & sludge with cracking whips they go
He lays his jacket with his luncheon bye
& drinks from horses footings when adry
They pass the maiden singing at her cow
& start the lark that roosted by the plough
That sings above them all the live long day
& on they drive and hollow care away

112.

(*Enter MARK ANTONY, and EROS.*)

ANTONY.   *Eros*, thou yet behold'st me?
EROS.   Ay, Noble Lord.
ANTONY.   Sometime we see a clowd that's Dragonish,
A vapour sometime, like a Beare, or Lyon,
A tower'd Cittadell, a pendant Rocke,
A forked Mountaine, or blew Promontorie
With Trees upon't, that nodde unto the world,
And mocke our eyes with Ayre. Thou hast seene these Signes,
They are blacke Vesper's Pageants.
EROS.   Ay, my Lord.
ANTONY.   That which is now a Horse, even with a thought
The Racke dislimns, and makes it indistinct
As water is in water.
EROS.   It does my Lord.

113.

Popular imagination links the Chinese Dragon to clouds, to the rainfall needed by farmers, and to great rivers. 'The earth couples with the dragon' is a common phrase for rain. About the sixth century, Chang Seng-yu executed a wall painting that depicted four Dragons. Viewers complained that he had left out their eyes. Annoyed, Chang picked up his brushes again and completed two of the twisted figures. Suddenly, 'the air was filled with thunder and lightning, the wall cracked and the Dragons ascended to heaven. But the other two eyeless Dragons remained in place'.

114.

Clouds take shape in the blue sky and gather
where flying bodies get tangled up together;
tiny clouds are borne along by breezes
till the moment when a stronger current rises.
Hills, for instance: the higher up the peak
the more industriously they seem to smoke;
wind blows these wisps on to the mountain tops
while they are still vague, evanescent strips
and there, heaped up in greater quantity,
they reveal themselves as a visible entity
trailing from snowy summits into the ether,
the empyrean spaces torn by wind and weather.
Steam rises from the sea, as becomes clear
when clothes on the shore absorb the salty air;
particles rise from rivers and wet slopes
while the sky, weighing upon them, packs them tight
and weaves them closely like a linen sheet.
Some come from space, as I've explained before,
their number infinite, their source obscure,
and these can travel at the speed of light.
No wonder the storm clouds, so fast and thick,
darkening fields and sea, slide up so quick
since from the blow-holes of the outer spheres,

as in our own windpipes, our glands and pores
the elements come and go, mysterious and opaque,
through ducts and channels, rooms and corridors
as if in a house of opening, closing doors.
As for the rain clouds, how they come to grow
and fall as rain on the drinking earth below -
a multitude of life-germs, water semen, floats
with cloud stuff and secretions of all sorts,
both swollen up, the fat clouds and whatever
solution is in the clouds themselves, cloud-water,
as our own bodies grow with the serum, gism,
sweat, whatever fluid is in the organism;
also they draw up brine with streaming sieves
when wind drives the clouds over the waves,
hoisting it from the surface in dripping fleeces
(same thing with bogs and other soggy places).
When all these water-sources come together
clouds discharge their excess moisture either
by ganging up in a bunch to crush each other
till tears flow; or else, blown thin by winds
and sun-struck, they give off drizzling rains
as wax held to a brazier melts and runs.
Sometimes the two things coincide, of course,
the violent pushing and the rushing wind-force,
and then you get a cloudburst which persists
with clouds upon clouds, tempests upon tempests
pouring out of the heavens, soaking the smoky air
while the earth breathes back in bubbles everywhere.

115.

– Tell me, you difficult man, whom do you love best: your father,
        your mother, your sister, your brother?
– I have no father or mother, sister or brother.
– Friends?

– You use a word whose meaning, to this day, is unknown to me.
– Your country?
– I hardly know in which latitude it lies.
– Beauty?
– I would serve her gratefully, were she a goddess and immortal.
– Gold?
– I detest it as much as you hate your God.
– What do you love, then, strangest of strangers?
– The clouds … I love the clouds that pass … there … and
    there … peerless, ineffable clouds!

116.

In public squares laid out near the gardens where the workers (or creators, as they had begun to call themselves) went for recreation, high white walls resembling white books opened against the dark sky. The squares were always full of crowds, and it was here that the creators' commune brought the latest news to the public by means of shadow printing on shadow books, projecting the appropriate shadow text by means of the projector's dazzling eye. News flashes about Planet Earth, the activities of that great union of workers' communes known as the United Encampments of Asia, poetry and the instantaneous inspirations of members, breakthroughs in science, notifications for relatives and next of kin, directives from the soviets. Those who were inspired by these shadow-book communications were able to go off for a moment, write down their own inspirations, and half an hour later see their messages projected onto those walls in shadow letters by means of the light lens. In cloudy weather the clouds themselves were used as screens, the latest news projected directly onto them. Many people requested that news of their deaths be flashed onto the clouds. For holiday celebrations there were 'shot paintings'. Smoke grenades of different colors were fired into the sky at various points. Eyes, for instance, were shots of blue smoke, the mouth a streak of scarlet smoke, hair of silver, and against the cloudless blue background of the heavens a familiar face would suddenly appear, marking a celebration in honour of a popular leader.

117.

SOCRATES.   There is no Zeus.
STREPSIADES.   No Zeus! What are you saying? Who causes the
rain to fall? Answer me that!
SOCRATES.   The clouds, of course, those dear goddesses. And I can
prove it. Have you ever seen rain without clouds? Let us see if Zeus
can make rain out of a clear blue sky!
STREPSIADES.   By Apollo, this is powerfully argued! And there I
was, thinking that rain was Zeus making water, all over us, through a
sieve. So tell me: who makes the thunder, which is so bad for my
nerves?
SOCRATES.   The clouds, of course, when they roll over each
other.
STREPSIADES.   But how can this be, you craziest of men!
SOCRATES.   They get bloated with water, and hanging up there
they have no choice but to keep moving, so they bump and crash into
each other. Which makes them even more bloated. And then they
burst. Bang bang.
STREPSIADES.   But surely it is Zeus who keeps them moving?
SOCRATES.   Not at all; it is the aerial Whirlwind.
STREPSIADES.   Ah, the aerial Whirlwind! That explains
everything. So Zeus no longer exists, and the aerial Whirlwind reigns
in his stead? But you have still not explained what makes the
thunder roll …
SOCRATES.   As I keep saying, the clouds bump against each other
when they are full of rain, and being inordinately swollen, they burst
with a big noise. Bang.
STREPSIADES.   How can anyone credit such nonsense?

118.

It may perhaps give some idea of one of these bright and silvery days
in spring, when at noon large garish clouds, surcharged with hail or
sleet, sweep with their broad shadows the fields, woods, and hills; and
by their depths enhance the value of the vivid greens and yellows so
peculiar to the season. The *natural history*, if the expression may be
used, of the skies, which are so particularly marked in the hail squalls

at this time of year is this: the clouds accumulate in very large and dense masses, and from their loftiness seem to move but slowly; immediately upon these large clouds appear numerous opaque patches, which, however, are only small clouds passing rapidly before them, and consisting of isolated pieces, detached probably from the larger cloud. These, floating much nearer the earth, may perhaps fall in with a stronger current of wind, which as well as their comparative lightness, causes them to move with greater rapidity; hence they are called by wind-millers and sailors, *messengers*, being always the forerunners of bad weather. They float about midway in what may be termed lanes of the clouds; and from being so situated are almost uniformly in shadow, receiving only a reflected light from the clear blue sky immediately above, and which descends perpendicularly upon them into these lanes. In passing over the bright parts of the large clouds, they appear as 'darks'; but in passing the shadowed parts they assume a grey, a pale, or lurid hue.

119.

Vapour brought to us by such a wind must have been generated in countries lying to the South and East of our island. It is therefore probably in the extensive vallies watered by the Meuse, the Moselle, and the Rhine, if not from the more distant Elbe, with the Oder and Weser, that the water rises, in the midst of sunshine, which is soon afterwards to form *our* clouds, and pour down in *our* Thunder-showers. And this island, in all probability, does the same office for Ireland: nay, the Eastern for the Western counties of South Britain.

120.

Ireland! Ireland! That cloud in the West! That coming storm!

121.

Beware of the oak; it draws the stroke.
Avoid the ash; it courts the flash;
Creep under a thorn; it may save you from harm.

122.

If it sinks from the north
It will double its wrath.
If it sinks from the south
It will open its mouth.
If it sinks from the west
It is never at rest.
If it sinks from the east
It will leave us in peace.

123.

Last night we had a thunderstorm in style.
The wild lightning streaked the airs,
As though my God fell down a pair of stairs.
The thunder boomed and bounded all the while;
All cried and sat by water-side and stile –
To mop our brow had been our chief of cares.
I lay in bed with a Voltairean smile,
The terror of good, simple guilty pairs,
And made this rondeau in ironic style,
Last night we had a thunderstorm in style.
Our God the Father fell down-stairs,
The stark blue lightning went its flight, the while,
The very rain you might have heard a mile –
The strenuous faithful buckled to their prayers.

124.

1 January 1766. As I have for these 30 years kept a sort of Diary of the Weather & Journal of other Things, being as someone justly enough calls it, The Importance of a Man to his own Self, I shall, till I am tired of it, transcribe from my Almanacks the contents of them, & so run over the last year, & be ashamed of the Manner in which it has passed.

125.

18 July 1773. Loud thunder shower. Mrs Snooke of Ringmer near Lewes had a coach-horse killed by this tempest: the horse was at grass just before the house.

126.

A stone is a diary of the weather, like a meteorological concentrate. A stone is nothing but weather itself, excluded from atmospheric space and banished to functional space. In order to understand this, you must imagine that all geological changes and displacements can be resolved completely into elements of weather. In this sense, meteorology is more fundamental than mineralogy, which it embraces, washes over, ages, and to which it gives meaning. A stone is an impressionistic diary of weather, accumulated by millions of years of disasters – not only of the past, but also of the future: for it contains periodicity.

127.

('Epitaph on the Stanton Harcourt Lovers, who being with many others at harvest work, were both in an instant killed by lightning on the last day of July 1718')

> Here lye two poor Lovers, who had the mishap
> Tho' very chaste people, to die of a Clap.

128.

Ah in the thunder air
how still the trees are!

And the lime-tree, lovely and tall, every leaf silent
hardly looses even a last breath of perfume.

And the ghostly, creamy coloured little tree of leaves
white, ivory white among the rambling greens
how evanescent, variegated elder, she hesitates on the green grass
as if, in another moment, she would disappear
with all her grace of foam!

And the larch that is only a column, it goes up too tall to see:
and the balsam-pines that are blue with the grey-blue blueness
     of things from the sea,
and the young copper beech, its leaves red-rosy at the ends
how still they are together, they stand so still
in the thunder air, all strangers to one another
as the green grass glows upwards, strangers in the silent garden.

129.

I kissed her, and my baby brother, and was very sorry then; but not
sorry to go away, for the gulf between us was there, and the parting
was there, every day. And it is not so much the embrace she gave me,
that lives in my mind, though it was as fervent as could be, as what
followed the embrace.

    I was in the carrier's cart when I heard her calling to me. I looked
out, and she stood at the garden-gate alone, holding her baby up in
her arms for me to see. It was cold still weather; and not a hair of her
head, nor a fold of her dress, was stirred, as she looked intently at me,
holding up her child.

    So I lost her. So I saw her afterwards, in my sleep at school – a
silent presence near my bed – looking at me with the same intent
face – holding up her baby in her arms.

130.

20 July 1778. Much thunder. Some people in the village were struck
down by the storm, but not hurt. The stroke seemed to them like a
violent push or shove. The ground is well-soaked. Wheat much
lodged. Frogs migrate from the ponds.

131.

23 September 1783. Black snails lie out, & copulate. Vast swagging clouds.

132.

Under this window in stormy weather
I marry this man and woman together;
Let none but Him who rules the thunder
Put this man and woman asunder.

133.

The summer of the year 1783 was an amazing and portentous one, and full of horrible phaenomena; for, besides the alarming meteors and tremendous thunder-storms that affrighted and distressed the different counties of this kingdom, the peculiar haze, or smokey fog, that prevailed for many weeks in this island, and in every part of Europe, and even beyond its limits, was a most extraordinary appearance, unlike any thing known within the memory of man. By my journal I find that I had noticed this strange occurrence from June 23 to July 20 inclusive, during which period the wind varied to every quarter without making any alteration in the air. The sun, at noon, looked as blank as a clouded moon, and shed a rust-coloured ferruginous light on the ground, and floors of rooms; but was particularly lurid and blood-coloured at rising and setting. All the time the heat was so intense that butchers' meat could hardly be eaten on the day after it was killed; and the flies swarmed so in the lanes and hedges that they rendered the horses half frantic, and riding irksome. The country people began to look with a superstitious awe at the red, louring aspect of the sun; and indeed there was reason for the most enlightened person to be apprehensive; for, all the while, Calabria and part of the isle of Sicily, were torn and convulsed with earthquakes; and about that juncture a volcano sprung out of the sea on the coast of Norway. On this occasion Milton's noble simile of the sun, in his first book of *Paradise Lost*, frequency occurred to my mind; and it is indeed particularly applicable, because, towards the

end, it alludes to a superstitious kind of dread, with which the minds
of men are always impressed by such strange and unusual
phaenomena.

> as when the Sun new ris'n
> Looks through the Horizontal misty air
> Shorn of his beams, or from behind the Moon
> In dim Eclips disastrous twilight sheds
> On half the nations, and with fear of change
> Perplexes Monarchs. Dark'n'd so, yet shon
> Above them all th' Arch Angel; but his face
> Deep scars of Thunder had intrencht, and care
> Sat on his faded cheek.

134.

Hidden, oh hidden
in the high fog
the house we live in,
beneath the magnetic rock,
rain-, rainbow-ridden,
where blood-black
bromelias, lichens,
owls, and the lint
of the waterfalls cling,
familiar, unbidden.

In a dim age
of water
the brook sings loud
from a rib cage
of giant fern; vapor
climbs up the thick growth
effortlessly, turns back,
holding them both,
house and rock,
in a private cloud.

At night, on the roof,
blind drops crawl
and the ordinary brown
owl gives us proof
he can count:
five times – always five –
he stamps and takes off
after the fat frogs that,
shrilling for love,
clamber and mount.

House, open house
to the white dew
and the milk-white sunrise
kind to the eyes,
to membership
of silver fish, mouse,
bookworms,
big moths; with a wall
for the mildew's
ignorant map;

darkened and tarnished
by the warm touch
of the warm breath,
maculate, cherished,
rejoice! For a later
era will differ.
(O difference that kills,
or intimidates, much
of all our small shadowy
life!) Without water

the great rock will stare
unmagnetized, bare,
no longer wearing
rainbows or rain,
the forgiving air

and the high fog gone;
the owls will move on
and the several
waterfalls shrivel
in the steady sun.

135.

29 June 1783. The Boethian atmosphere I have breathed these six days
past ... So long, in a country not subject to fogs, we have been cover'd
with one of the thickest I remember. We never see the Sun but shorn
of his beams, the trees are scarce discernable at a mile's distance, he
sets with the face of a red-hot salamander, and rises (as I learn from
report), with the same complexion. Such a Phaenomenon at the end
of June has occasioned much speculation among the Cognoscenti at
this place. Some fear to go to bed, expecting an Earthquake, some
declare that he neither rises nor sets where he did, and assert with
great confidence that the day of Judgment is at hand. This is probable,
and I believe it myself, but for other reasons. In the mean time I
cannot discover in them, however alarmed, the symptoms even of a
temporary reformation. This very Sunday morning the pitchers of ale
have been carried into Silver-end as usual, the inhabitants perhaps
judging that they have more than ordinary need of that cordial at
such a juncture. It is however, seriously, a remarkable appearance, and
the only one of the kind that at this season of the year has fallen
under my notice. Signs in the heavens are predicted characters of the
last times; and in the course of the last 15 years I have been a witness
of many. The present obfuscation (if I may call it so) of all nature may
be rank'd perhaps amongst the most remarkable. But possibly it may
not be universal; in London, at least, where a dingey atmosphere is
frequent, it may be less observable.

136.

15 July, 1783. I am tired of this weather – it parches the leaves, makes
the turf crisp, claps the doors, blows the papers about, and keeps one
in a constant mist that gives no dew, but might as well be smoke. The

sun sets like a pewter plate red hot; and then in a moment appears the moon, at a distance, of the same complexion, just as the same orb, in a moving picture, serves for both. I wish modern philosophers had not disturbed all our ideas! Two hundred years ago celestial and terrestrial affairs hung together, and if a country was out of order it was comfortable to think that the planets ordered, or sympathised with its ails. A sun shorn of his beams, and a moon that only serves to make darkness visible, are mighty homogenial to a distracted State; and when their Ministry is changed every twelve hours, without allaying the heat or mending the weather, Father Holinshed would have massed the whole in the Casualties of the Reign, and expected no better till he was to tap a new accession.

As I have meditated so profoundly on the season, you will perceive, Madam, that I had nothing else to talk of . . .

137.

Fog everywhere. Fog up the river, where it flows among green aits and meadows; fog down the river, where it rolls defiled among the tiers of shipping, and the waterside pollutions of a great (and dirty) city. Fog on the Essex marshes, fog on the Kentish heights. Fog creeping into the cabooses of collier-brigs; fog lying out on the yards, and hovering in the rigging of great ships; fog drooping on the gunwales of barges and small boats. Fog in the eyes and throats of ancient Greenwich pensioners, wheezing by the firesides of their wards; fog in the stem and bowl of the afternoon pipe of the wrathful skipper, down in his close cabin; fog cruelly pinching the toes and fingers of his shivering little 'prentice boy on deck. Chance people on the bridges peeping over the parapets into a nether sky of fog, with fog all round them, as if they were up in a balloon, and hanging in the misty clouds.

Gas looming through the fog in divers places in the streets, much as the sun may, from the spongy fields, be seen to loom by husbandman and ploughboy. Most of the shops lighted two hours before their time – as the gas seems to know, for it has a haggard and unwilling look.

138.

Why is it that the life that overflows in Dickens seems to me always to go on in the morning, or in the very earliest hours of the afternoon at most, and in a vast apartment that appears to have windows, large, uncurtained and rather unwashed windows, on all sides at once? Why is it that in George Eliot the sun sinks forever to the west, and the shadows are long, and the afternoon wanes, and the trees vaguely rustle, and the colour of the day is much inclined to yellow? Why is it that in Charlotte Brontë we move through an endless autumn? Why is it that in Jane Austen we sit quite resigned in an arrested spring? Why does Hawthorne give us the afternoon hour later than any one else? — oh, late, late, quite uncannily late, and as if it were always winter outside?

But I am wasting the very minutes I pretended, at the start, to cherish, and am only sustained through my levity by seeing you watch for the time of day or season of the year or state of the weather that I shall fasten upon the complicated clock-face of Thackeray. I do, I think, see his light also – see it very much as the light (a different thing from the mere dull dusk) of rainy days in 'residential' streets; but we are not, after all, talking of him, and, though Balzac's waiting power has proved itself, this half-century, immense, I must not too much presume upon it.

The question of the colour of Balzac's air and the time of *his* day would indeed here easily solicit our ingenuity – were I at liberty to say more than one thing about it. It is rich and thick, the mixture of sun and shade diffused through the *Comédie Humaine* – a mixture richer and thicker, and representing an absolutely greater quantity of '*atmosphere*', than we shall find prevailing within the compass of any other suspended frame.

139.

Profound boredom, drifting here and there in the abysses of our existence like a muffling fog, removes all things and men and onself along with it into a remarkable indifference. This boredom reveals being as a whole.

140.

I do not know much about gods; but I think that the river
Is a strong brown god – sullen, untamed and intractable,
Patient to some degree, at first recognised as a frontier;
Useful, untrustworthy, as a conveyer of commerce;
Then only a problem confronting the builder of bridges.
The problem once solved, the brown god is almost forgotten
By the dwellers in cities – ever, however, implacable,
Keeping his seasons and rages, destroyer, reminder
Of what men choose to forget. Unhonoured, unpropitiated
By worshippers of the machine, but waiting, watching and waiting.
His rhythm was present in the nursery bedroom,
In the rank ailanthus of the April dooryard,
In the smell of grapes on the autumn table,
And the evening circle in the winter gaslight.

The river is within us, the sea is all about us;
The sea is the land's edge also, the granite
Into which it reaches, the beaches where it tosses
Its hints of earlier and other creation:
The starfish, the horseshoe crab, the whale's backbone;
The pools where it offers to our curiosity
The more delicate algae and the sea anemone.
It tosses up our losses, the torn seine,
The shattered lobsterpot, the broken oar
And the gear of foreign dead men. The sea has many voices,
Many gods and many voices.
                              The salt is on the briar rose,
The fog is in the fir trees.
                              The sea howl
And the sea yelp, are different voices
Often together heard: the whine in the rigging,
The menace and caress of wave that breaks on water,
The distant rote in the granite teeth,
And the wailing warning from the approaching headland
Are all sea voices, and the heaving groaner
Rounded homewards, and the seagull:
And under the oppression of the silent fog

The tolling bell
Measures time not our time, rung by the unhurried
Ground swell, a time
Older than the time of chronometers, older
Than time counted by anxious worried women
Lying awake, calculating the future,
Trying to unweave, unwind, unravel
And piece together the past and the future,
Between midnight and dawn, when the past is all deception,
The future futureless, before the morning watch
When time stops and time is never ending;
And the ground swell, that is and was from the beginning,
Clangs
The bell.

141.

Words … interpose themselves so much between our Understandings, and the Truth, which it would contemplate and apprehend, that like the *Medium* through which visible Objects pass, their Obscurity and Disorder does not seldom cast a mist before our Eyes.

142.

It was raining that day, a chilly rain, and mist floated in the air as His Majesty stepped out onto the balcony to make his speech. Next to him stood only a handful of soaked, depressed dignitaries – the rest were in prison or had fled the capital. There was no crowd, only the Palace servants and some soldiers from the Imperial Guard standing at the edge of an empty courtyard. His August Majesty expressed his compassion for the starving provinces and said that he would not neglect any chance to keep the Empire developing fruitfully. He also thanked the army for its loyalty, praised his subjects, encouraged them and wished them good luck. But he spoke so quietly that through the steady rain one could hardly make out individual words. And know, my friend, that I will take this memory to the grave with me, because I can still hear how His

Majesty's voice breaks, and I can see how tears stream down his venerable face. And then, yes, then, for the first time, I thought to myself that everything was really coming to an end. That on this rainy day all life is seeping away, we are covered with cold, clinging fog, and the moon and Jupiter have stopped in the seventh and the twelfth houses to form a square.

143.

I've seen things you people wouldn't believe.
Attack ships on fire off the shoulder of Orion.
I watched C-beams glitter in the dark near the Tannhäuser Gate.
All those moments will be lost in time, like tears in rain.
Time to die.

144.

In the courtyard where I watch it fall, the rain comes down at several different speeds. In the middle it is a delicate and threadbare curtain (or a mesh), an implacable but relatively slow descent of quite small drops, a never-ending languid precipitation, an intense fragment of pure meteor. A little away from the walls on left and right heavier drops fall separately, more noisily. Some look the size of a grain of corn, others a pea, others almost a marble. On the parapets and balustrades of the window the rain runs horizontally, while on the underside of these obstacles it hangs down in convex lozenges. It streams in a thin sheet over the entire surface of a little zinc roof directly below me – a pattern of watered silk, in the various currents, from the imperceptible bosses and undulations of the surface. From the adjoining gutter, where it flows with the contention of a deep but only slightly inclined stream, it suddenly plunges in a perfectly vertical, coarsely braided stream to the ground, where it breaks and rebounds in shining needles.

Each of these forms has its own particular speed and gait; each elicits a particular sound. The whole thing is intensely alive in the manner of a complicated mechanism, as precise as it is random, a clockwork whose spring is the weight of a given mass of precipitated vapour.

The ringing of the vertical threads on the pavement, the gurgling of the gutters, the tiny gong beats multiply and resonate all at once in a consort without monotony, and not without delicacy.

And when the spring is unwound, some of the gears continue to function for a while, getting slower and slower, until the whole machinery stops. Then, if the sun comes out again, the whole thing is erased, the brilliant apparatus evaporates: it has rained.

145.

And outside it's raining and raining and doesn't look as though it will ever stop. Which I do not mind in the least. I am sitting inside, dry, and am only embarrassed to be eating an opulent *Gabelfrühstück* in front of the house-painter who at this moment is standing on the scaffolding outside my window, and is spattering the windows unnecessarily because he is furious at the rain which has let up a little, and furious at the amount of butter I am putting on my bread. However, that too is probably my imagination, since he is no doubt 100 times less concerned about me than I am about him. No, now he really is hard at work, in the pouring rain and lightning ...

146.

In making a film of atmosphere, I found that you could not stick to the script and that the script should not get too detailed. In this case, the rain itself dictated its own literature and guided the camera into secret wet paths we had never dreamed of when we outlined the film. It was an exceptionally difficult subject to tackle. Many artistic problems were actually technical problems and vice versa. Film experience in photographing rain was extremely limited because a cameraman normally stops filming when it begins to rain. When *Rain* was finished and shown in Paris in 1929 the French critics called it a *ciné-poème* and its structure is actually more that of a poem than the prose of *The Bridge*. Its object is to show the changing face of a city, Amsterdam, during a shower.

The film opens with clear sunshine on houses, canals and people in the streets. A slight wind rises and the first drops of rain splash into the canals. The shower comes down harder and the people hasten about their business under the protection of capes and umbrellas. The shower ends. The last drops fall and the city's life returns to normal. The only continuity in *Rain* is the onset, progress and end of this shower. There are neither titles nor dialogue. Its effects are intended as purely visual. The actors are the rain, the raindrops, the wet people, dark clouds, glistening reflections moving over wet asphalt, and so forth. The diffused light on the dark houses along the black canals produced an effect that I never expected. And the whole film produces in the spectator a very personal and subjective vision. As in Verlaine's lines:

Il pleure dans mon coeur
Comme il pleut sur la ville;
Quelle est cette langueur
Qui pénètre mon coeur?
Ô bruit doux de la pluie
Par terre et sur les toits!

At that time I lived with and for the rain. I tried to imagine how everything I saw would look in the rain – and on the screen. It was part game, part obsession, part action … I never moved without my camera – it was with me in the office, laboratory, street, train. I lived with it and when I slept it was on my bedside table so that if it was raining when I woke I could film the studio window over my bed. Some of the best shots of raindrops along the slanted studio windows were actually taken from my bed when I woke up. All the new problems in this film sharpened my observations and forced me to relax the rigid and over-analytical method of filming I had used hitherto. With the swiftly shifting rhythm and light of the rain, sometimes changing within a few seconds, my filming had to be defter and more spontaneous.

It took me about four months to get the footage I needed … The rain itself was a moody actress who had to be humoured and who refused anything but a natural make-up. I found that none of the new colour-corrective film emulsions on the market were suitable for my rain problems. The old rapid Agfa films with no colour-correction at all, and used without a filter, gave the best results. All lenses were used with a fully opened diaphragm because most of the work was done with a minimum of light (…)

In *Rain* I had to remind myself constantly that rain is wet – so you must keep the screen dripping with wetness – make the audience feel damp and not just dampness. When they think they can't get any wetter, *double* the wetness, show the raindrops falling into the water of the canal – make it super-wet. I was so happy when I noticed at one of the first screenings of the finished film that the audience looked around for their raincoats and were surpised to find the weather dry and clear when they came out of the theatre.

I had to make sure that the sunlight which began and ended the film showed its typical differences. You have to catch the distinction between the rich strong enveloping sunlight before rain and the strange dreamy yellow light afterwards.

Rain taught me a great deal about film emotion.

147.

The tortoise is a truly emblematic creature – note its firm stance and panegyric posture. We salute its longevity: moving without haste, its existence unfolds across a thousand years. And let us not forget the prophetic powers of its shell, curved in the image of the celestial vault and reproducing all its variations. When rubbed with ink and dried in the fire, it reveals as clearly as the signs of the sky itself the calm or stormy contours of future weather.

148.

My Lady Dedlock has been down at what she calls, in familiar conversation, her 'place' in Lincolnshire. The waters are out in Lincolnshire. An arch of the bridge in the park has been sapped and sopped away. The adjacent low-lying ground, for half a mile in breadth, is a stagnant river, with melancholy trees for islands in it, and a surface punctured all over, all day long, with falling rain. My Lady Dedlock's 'place' has been extremely dreary. The weather for many a day and night has been so wet that the trees seem wet through, and the soft loppings and prunings of the woodman's axe can make no crash or crackle as they fall. The deer, looking soaked, leave quagmires, where they pass. The shot of a rifle loses its sharpness in the moist air, and its smoke moves in a tardy little cloud towards the green rise, coppice-topped, that makes a background for the falling rain. The view from my Lady Dedlock's own windows is alternately a lead-coloured view, and a view in Indian ink. The vases on the stone terrace in the foreground catch the rain all day; and the heavy drops fall, drip, drip, drip, upon the broad flagged pavement, called from old time the Ghost's Walk, all night. On Sundays the little church in the park is mouldy; the oaken pulpit breaks out into a cold sweat; and there is a general smell and taste as of the ancient Dedlocks in their graves. My Lady Dedlock (who is childless), looking out in the early twilight from her boudoir at a keeper's lodge, and seeing the light of a fire upon the latticed panes, and smoke rising from the chimney, and a child, chased by a woman, running out into the rain to meet the shining figure of a wrapped-up man coming through the gate, has been put quite out of temper. My Lady Dedlock says she has been 'bored to death.'

149.

Sad is the burying in the sunshine,
But bless'd is the corpse that goeth home in rain.

150.

and the rain has commenced its delicate lament over the orchards

an enormous window morning and the wind, the beautiful
    desperation of a tree
fighting off strangulation, and my bed has an ugly calm

151.

Slow, slow, fresh fount, keepe time with my salt tears;
Yet slower, yet, O faintly, gentle springs:
List to the heavy part the musique beares:
    Woe weepes out her division, when shee sings.
      Droup hearbs and flowres,
      Fall, grief, in showres;
      Our beauties are not ours:
        O, I could still,
(Like melting snow upon some craggie hill)
      Drop, drop, drop, drop,
Since nature's pride is now a wither'd daffodil.

152.

Is it any surprise that colour should play such a very important part
in modern art? Romanticism is a child of the North, and the North is
a colourist; dreams and fairy tales are children of the mist. England
(that home of fanatical colourists), Flanders and half of France are
plunged in fog; Venice herself lies steeped in her lagoons.

    As for Spaniards, they are painters of contrasts rather than
colourists. The South is a naturalist; for here nature is so beautiful, so
bright, that nothing is left for man to desire, and he can find nothing
more beautiful to invent than what he sees. Here art belongs to the
open air; but a few hundred leagues to the north you will find the deep
dreams of the atelier, and the eye of fantasy is lost in horizons of grey.

153.

The rain now came down heavily, but they pursued their path with
alacrity, the produce of the several fields between which the lane
wound its way being indicated by the peculiar character of the sound
emitted by the falling drops. Sometimes a soaking hiss proclaimed
that they were passing by a pasture, then a patter would show that the
rain fell upon some large-leafed root crop, then a paddling plash
announced the naked arable, the low sound of the wind in their ears
rising and falling with each pace they took.

154.

look between the rain
the drops are insular
try to remember before you were born

155.

     They sing their dearest songs—
     He, she, all of them—yea,
     Treble and tenor and bass,
          And one to play;
     With the candles mooning each face.…
          Ah, no; the years O!
How the sick leaves reel down in throngs!

     They clear the creeping moss—
     Elders and juniors—aye,
     Making the pathways neat
          And the garden gay;
     And they build a shady seat.…
          Ah, no; the years, the years,
See, the white storm-birds wing across.

     They are blithely breakfasting all—
     Men and maidens—yea,
     Under the summer tree,
          With a glimpse of the bay,
     While pet fowl come to the knee.…
          Ah, no; the years O!
And the rotten rose is ript from the wall.

     They change to a high new house,
     He, she, all of them—aye,
     Clocks and carpets and chairs
          On the lawn all day,
     And brightest things that are theirs.…
          Ah, no; the years, the years;
Down their carved names the rain-drop ploughs.

156.

Bored with the town, our rain god pours his pitcher of torrential dark
over the next-door boneyard's pale people, and threads mortality
through the fog-bound faubourgs.

Revolving her wasted furious body, the cat roots for a bed on the
floorboards; thin voice lonesome as a cold ghost, the soul of an old
poet roams the gutters...

The great bell mourns, and from the grate a smoking log plays falsetto
to the rheumy clock, while in a pack of malodorous cards

(fatal heirloom of some hydroptic aunt), the queen of spades and
handsome knave of hearts keep up dark gossip round their dead
heart-throbs.

157.

The weather, you know, has not been balmy; I am now reduced to
think – and am at last content to talk – of the weather. Pride must
have a fall.

158.

He often delighted to say of Edmund Burke, 'that you could not stand
five minutes with that man beneath a shed while it rained, but you
must be convinced you had been standing with the greatest man you
had ever yet seen.'

159.

It is commonly observed, that when two Englishmen meet, their first
talk is of the weather; they are in haste to tell each other, what each
must already know, that it is hot or cold, bright or cloudy, windy or
calm.

There are, among the numerous lovers of subtilties and paradoxes,
some who derive the civil institutions of every country from its

climate, who impute freedom and slavery to the temperature of the air, can fix the meridian of vice and virtue, and tell at what degree of latitude we are to expect courage or timidity, knowledge or ignorance.

From these dreams of idle speculation, a slight survey of life, and a little knowledge of history, are sufficient to awaken any inquirer, whose ambition of distinction has not overpowered his love of truth. Forms of government are seldom the result of much deliberation; they are framed by chance in popular assemblies, or in conquered countries, by despotick authority. Laws are often occasional, often capricious, made always by a few, and sometimes by a single voice. Nations have changed their characters; slavery is now no where more patiently endured, than in countries once inhabited by the zealots of liberty. But national customs can arise only from general agreement; they are not imposed, but chosen, and are continued only by the continuance of their cause. An Englishman's notice of the weather is the natural consequence of changeable skies and uncertain seasons. In many parts of the world, wet weather and dry are regularly expected at certain periods; but in our island every man goes to sleep, unable to guess whether he shall behold in the morning a bright or cloudy atmosphere, whether his rest shall be lulled by a shower, or broken by a tempest. We therefore rejoice mutually at good weather, as at an escape from something that we feared; and mutually complain of bad, as of the loss of something that we hoped. Such is the reason of our practice; and who shall treat it with contempt? Surely not the attendant on a court, whose business is to watch the looks of a being weak and foolish as himself, and whose vanity is to recount the names of men, who might drop into nothing, and leave no vacuity; nor the proprietor of funds, who stops his acquaintance in the street to tell him of the loss of half-a-crown; nor the inquirer after news, who fills his head with foreign events, and talks of skirmishes and sieges, of which no consequence will ever reach his hearers or himself.

The weather is a nobler and more interesting subject; it is the present state of the skies, and of the earth, on which plenty and famine are suspended, on which millions depend for the necessaries of life. The weather is frequently mentioned for another reason, less honourable to my dear countrymen. Our dispositions too frequently change with the colour of the sky; and when we find ourselves cheerful and good-natured, we naturally pay our acknowledgments to the powers of sunshine; or, if we sink into dulness and peevishness, look round the horizon for an excuse, and charge our discontent upon an easterly wind or a cloudy day. Surely nothing is more reproachful to a being endowed with reason, than to resign its powers to the influence of the air, and live in dependence on the weather and the wind, for the only blessings which nature has put into our power, tranquillity and benevolence. To look up to the sky for the nutriment of our bodies, is the condition of nature; to call upon the sun for peace and gaiety, or deprecate the clouds lest sorrow should overwhelm us, is the cowardice of idleness, and the idolatry of folly. Yet even in this age of inquiry and knowledge, when superstition is driven away, and omens and prodigies have lost their terrors, we find this folly countenanced by frequent examples.

Those that laugh at the portentous glare of a comet, and hear a crow with equal tranquillity from the right or left, will yet talk of times and situations proper for intellectual performances, will imagine the fancy exalted by vernal breezes, and the reason invigorated by a bright calm. If men who have given up themselves to fanciful credulity would confine their conceits in their own minds, they might regulate their lives by the barometer, with inconvenience only to themselves; but to fill the world with accounts of intellects subject to ebb and flow, of one genius that awakened in the spring, and another that ripened in the autumn, of one mind expanded in the summer, and of another concentrated in the winter, is no less dangerous than to tell children of bugbears and goblins.

160.

His decision, to choose a quite ordinary occupation and, if possible, become a country schoolteacher was one that I found difficult to understand at first. Since we – my brothers and sisters – often used analogies to explain to each other what we meant, I told him that when I thought of him as an elementary school teacher, with his philosophically trained mind, it seemed to me like someone using a precision instrument to open crates. Ludwig replied with an analogy which reduced me to silence: 'You remind me,' he said, 'of someone who is looking through a closed window and cannot explain to

himself the strange movements of a passer-by. He cannot tell what
sort of storm is raging out there, or that this person might only be
managing with great difficulty to stay on his feet.'

161.

The apparition   of these faces   in the crowd   :
Petals   on a wet, black   bough   .

162.

Full many a glorious morning have I seene,
Flatter the mountaine tops with sovereaine eie,
Kissing with golden face the meddowes greene,
Guilding pale streames with heavenly alcumy:
Anon permit the basest cloudes to ride
With ougly rack on his celestiall face,
And from the for-lorne world his visage hide
Stealing unseene to west with this disgrace:
Even so my Sunne one early morne did shine
With all-triumphant splendor on my brow,
But out, alack, he was but one houre mine;
The region cloude hath mask'd him from me now.
        Yet him for this, my love no whit disdaineth,
        Suns of the world may staine, when heaven's sun staineth.

163.

                    1.

Gently disintegrate me
Said nothing at all.

Is there still time to say
Said I myself lying
In a bower of bramble
Into which I have fallen.

Look through my eyes up
At blue with not anything
We could have ever arranged
Slowly taking place.

Above the spires of the fox
Gloves and above the bracken
Tops with their young heads
Recognising the wind,
The armies of the empty
Blue press me further
Into Zennor Hill.

If I half-close my eyes
The spiked light leaps in
And I am here as near
Happy as I will get
In the sailing afternoon.

2.

Enter a cloud. Between
The head of Zennor and
Gurnard's Head the long
Marine horizon makes
A blue wall or is it
A distant table-top
Of the far-off simple sea.

Enter a cloud. O cloud,
I see you entering from
Your west gathering yourself
Together into a white
Headlong. And now you move
And stream out of the Gurnard,
The west corner of my eye.

Enter a cloud. The cloud's
Changing shape is crossing

Slowly only an inch
Above the line of the sea.
Now nearly equidistant
Between Zennor and Gurnard's
Head, an elongated
White anvil is sailing
Not wanting to be a symbol.

3.

Said nothing at all.

And proceeds with no idea
Of destination along
The sea bearing changing
Messages. Jean in London,
Lifting a cup, looking
Abstractedly out through
Her Hampstead glass will never
Be caught by your new shape
Above the chimneys. Jean,
Jean, do you not see
This cloud has been thought of
And written on Zennor Hill.

4.

The cloud is going beyond
What I can see or make.
Over up-country maybe
Albert Strick stops and waves
Caught in the middle of teeling
Broccoli for the winter.
The cloud is not there yet.

From Gurnard's Head to Zennor
Head the level line
Crosses my eyes lying
On buzzing Zennor Hill.

The cloud is only a wisp
And gone behind the Head.
It is funny I got the sea's
Horizontal slightly surrealist.
Now when I raise myself
Out of the bracken I see
The long empty blue
Between the fishing Gurnard
And Zennor. It was a cloud
The language at my time's
Disposal made use of.

5.

Thank you. And for your applause.
It has been a pleasure. I
Have never enjoyed speaking more.
May I also thank the real ones
Who have made this possible.
First, the cloud itself. And now
Gurnard's Head and Zennor
Head. Also recognise
How I have been helped
By Jean and Madron's Albert
Strick (He is a real man.)
And good words like brambles,
Bower, spiked, fox, anvil, teeling.

The bees you heard are from
A hive owned by my friend
Garfield down there below
In the house by Zennor Church.

The good blue sun is pressing
Me into Zennor Hill.

Gently disintegrate me
Said nothing at all.

164.

And thus did the Atmospherical Theatre play out, with its
transmutations & shifting of vapours, whether the rain-bearing
clouds of January riding over our heades like vast Carracks –
Atmosphere loaded & varnished with Bulging, dull-swelling
Bas-Relieve clouds bloated & pendulous, I style them *ubera caeli
fecunda*: sky cubbies or udders cloudy; they enclos'd & stufft the
whole visible Hemisphere in colour like Lead-vapours or a tall Fresco
ceiling, or marbled veined grotto.

165.

Digressions, incontestably, are the sunshine; — they are the life, the
soul of reading; – take them out of this book for instance, — you
might as well take the book along with them; — one cold eternal
winter would reign in every page of it.

166.

Hallam and Tennyson at a meeting of the Apostles (1829), lying on
the ground in order to laugh less painfully, when Spedding imitated
the sun going behind a cloud and coming out again – *Desmond
MacCarthy to me (Garrick Club, June 1943).*

167.

'Twas so, I saw thy birth: That drowsie Lake
From her faint bosome breath'd thee, the disease
Of her sick waters, and Infectious Ease.
      But, now at Even,
      Too grosse for heaven,
Thou fall'st in tears, and weep'st for thy mistake.

Ah! it is so with me; oft have I prest
Heaven with a lazie breath, but fruitles this
Pierc'd not; Love only can with quick accesse

> Unlock the way,
>   When all else stray,
> The smoke, and Exhalations of the brest.

> Yet, if as thou doest melt, and with thy traine
> Of drops make soft the Earth, my eyes could weep
> O'er my hard heart, that's bound up and asleep;
>   Perhaps at last
>   (Some such showres past)
> My God would give a Sun-shine after raine.

168.

1 June 1711. At night. I never felt so hot a day as this since I was born. I dined with Lady Betty Germain, and there was the young Earl of Berkeley and his fine lady. I never saw her before, nor think her near so handsome as she passes for.—After dinner Mr. Bertue would not let me put ice in my wine; but said my Lord Dorchester got the bloody-flux with it, and that it was the worst thing in the world. Thus are we plagued, thus are we plagued; yet I have done it five or six times this summer, and was but the drier and the hotter for it. Nothing makes me so excessively peevish as hot weather. Lady Berkeley after dinner clapt my hat on another lady's head, and she in roguery put it upon the rails. I minded them not; but in two minutes they called me to the window, and Lady Carteret showed me my hat out of her window five doors off, where I was forced to walk to it, and pay her and old Lady Weymouth a visit, with some more beldames.

Then I went and drank coffee, and made one or two puns with Lord Pembroke, and designed to go to Lord Treasurer; but it was too late, and beside I was half broiled, and broiled without butter; for I never sweat after dinner, if I drink my wine. Then I sat an hour with Lady Betty Butler at tea, and every thing made me hotter and drier. Then I walkt home, and was here by ten, so miserably hot, that I was in as perfect a passion as ever I was in my life at the greatest affront or provocation. Then I sat an hour, till I was quite dry and cool enough to go swim; which I did, but with so much vexation, that I think I have given it over: for I was every moment disturbed by boats, rot them; and that puppy Patrick, standing ashore, would let them come within a yard or two, and then call sneakingly to them. The only comfort I proposed here in hot weather is gone; for there is no jesting with those boats after 'tis dark: I had none last night. I dived to dip my head, and held my cap on with both my hands, for fear of losing it. – Pox take the boats! Amen.

169.

I saw the sun, such was its radiance
    That I seemed to myself in a trance:
But elsewhere ocean roared,
    Mingled with the blood of men.

I saw the sun; at the sight I trembled,
    I was downcast and in dread:
My heart was grieved and greatly troubled:
    My soul was torn asunder.

I saw the sun, so saddened was I
    That my breath was nigh out of my body:
My tongue felt hard as timber and the world
    About me was bitter cold.

I never saw the sun again
    After that downcast day:
The underground waters closed over me then,
    And I turned, cold, from my torments.

170.

Every man has a rainy corner of his life, out of which foul weather proceeds, and follows after him.

171.

Then I went back into the house and wrote, It is midnight. The rain is beating on the windows. It was not midnight. It was not raining.

172.

In Tse'gihi,
In the house made of the dawn,
In the house made of the evening twilight,
In the house made of the dark cloud,
In the house made of the he-rain,
In the house made of the dark mist,
In the house made of the she-rain,
In the house made of pollen,
In the house made of grasshoppers,
Where the dark mist curtains the doorway,
The path to which is on the rainbow,
Where the zigzag lightning stands high on top,
Where the he-rain stands high on top,
Oh, male divinity!

With your moccasins of dark cloud, come to us.
With your leggings of dark cloud, come to us.
With your shirt of dark cloud, come to us.
With your head-dress of dark cloud, come to us.
With your mind enveloped in dark cloud, come to us.
With the dark thunder above you, come to us soaring.
With the shapen cloud at your feet, come to us soaring.
With the far darkness made of the dark cloud over your head, come
        to us soaring.
With the far darkness made of the he-rain over your head, come to
        us soaring.
With the far darkness made of the dark mist over your head, come to
        us soaring.
With the far darkness made of the she-rain over your head, come to
        us soaring.
With the zigzag lightning flung out on high over your head, come to
        us soaring.
With the rainbow hanging high over your head, come to us
        soaring.
With the far darkness made of the dark cloud on the ends of your
        wings, come to us soaring.

With the far darkness made of the he-rain on the ends of your wings,
   come to us soaring.
With the far darkness made of the dark mist on the ends of your
   wings, come to us soaring.
With the far darkness made of the she-rain on the ends of your
   wings, come to us soaring.
With the zigzag lightning flung out on high on the ends of your
   wings, come to us soaring.
With the rainbow hanging high on the ends of your wings, come to
   us soaring.
With the near darkness made of the dark cloud, of the he-rain, of the
   dark mist and of the she-rain, come to us.

173.

It's not a question of people of African descent having adapted to the
rain or in simpler language just gotten used to the watery
environment. It goes way beyond that. At times it seems like love.
Certainly homeopathy. In the town of Guapi, it had not rained for
three days. Then it pelted down, drumming on the roof, and everyone
shot outside. The young men played mini-football, slicing through
curtains of rain and skidding through puddles like ducks, while girls
and boys jumped into the swiftly moving river. 'In the rain?' Yes! ¡Es
más sabroso! It was as if we lived in a drought-stricken desert
suddenly relieved by rain, whereas in fact it rains like the dickens just
about every day. A broken gutter spouts a torrent down onto the
pavement. A girl and boy dance in it to the music coming from the
restaurant. She puts her hands on the wall and wags her bottom
under the waterspout. Later the boy lies in a trance on the pavement
in the same spot, rolling from side to side under the torrent for
several minutes. A pack of kids zigzag like a school of fish along the
street playing football and then dive into the rusting carcass of the
wheel-less truck parked outside the mayor's office, beating on it for all
they're worth and leaving the doors open as a parting gesture.
Marsella scoots outside to get on her bike. No raincoat, no umbrella.
And before peddling off in the pelting rain, she stoops over to scoop a
bucket of water from a baby's plastic bathtub by the front gate and

pour it over her head. Her mother comes in from two hours hunched over in an open launch thumping on the ocean's waves in a massive downpour. First thing she does is to bathe in the rainwater brimming over a tank in the backyard.

At Santa Barbara rain came down in torrents starting around five in the morning. I see kids playing basketball at 6.30 in the deluge. A girl aged about ten in a white singlet, black skirt and rubber sandals stretches out belly-down on the cement of the basketball court for at least two minutes enjoying the rain. Now she gets up. Tries to shoot a basket but can only get the ball up a few feet and so goes to paddle in the ankle-deep water of the drainage channel at the edge of the court after which she jumps in with both feet so as to make a splash, which she repeats again and again. A young guy in a bright yellow shirt comes and sits by her in the pouring rain with his feet in the water running along the drain. Now she has her sandals off as she walks up and down the drain with giant steps feeling the water running against her. She stoops to splash water over her face.

Upriver at Santa Maria the same water alchemy. A man works all day diving into the river excavating the bottom in search of gold. He is a fish. Immersed in moving water two to three metres down in the gloom. When he emerges, he immediately washes himself vigorously in the same water. Wendy Sulay, aged eight, comes home from the mine where she's been working along with maybe ten other kids after school, and dripping wet in the rain, we go straight to the river where we do the *largo*, the long one, which means wade out to where the current is strongest and be swept one person behind the other in a dizzying arc, bobbing like dolphins over the boulders to return almost where we started, thanks to the bend in the river. Surfing! Then there's the *tambor*, when in a circle of kids, you stand a bit more than knee-high and stamp down hard. An orange bubble swells up, and you clap the palm of your hand down pretty fast but gentle onto it as it gets close to the surface, and a great boom sounds. Magic!

And in the riverside town of Guapi surrounded by water but especially from the grey skies above, in all this water, I see a couple of young men struggling with a two-wheeled wooden cart neatly laden with big blue bottles of WATER FOR SALE, brought all the way from the great port of Buenaventura way north and from God knows where before that.

174.

Death is before me today like the passing of rain when a man returns from an expedition.

175.

Sometimes the rain-charm operates through the dead. Thus in New Caledonia the rain-makers blackened themselves all over, dug up a dead body, took the bones to a cave, jointed them, and hung the skeleton over some Taro leaves. Water was poured over the skeleton to run down on the leaves. They believed that the soul of the deceased took up the water, converted it into rain, and showered it down again. In Russia, if common report may be believed, it is not long since the peasants of any district that chanced to be afflicted with drought used to dig up the corpse of someone who had drunk himself to death and sink it in the nearest swamp or lake, fully persuaded that this would ensure the fall of the needed rain.

In 1868 the prospect of a bad harvest, caused by a prolonged drought, induced the inhabitants of a village in the Tarashchansk district to dig up the body of a Raskolnik, or Dissenter, who had died in the preceding December. Some of the party beat the corpse, or what was left of it, about the head, exclaiming, 'Give us Rain!' while others poured water on it through a sieve. Here the pouring of water through a sieve seems plainly an imitation of a shower, and reminds us of the manner in which Strepsiades in Aristophanes imagined that rain was made by Zeus. Sometimes, in order to procure rain, the Toradjas make an appeal to the pity of the dead. Thus in the village of Kalingooa there is the grave of a famous chief, the grandfather of the present ruler. When the land suffers from unseasonable drought, the people go to this grave, pour water on it, and say, 'O grandfather, have pity on us; if it is your will that this year we should eat, then give rain.' After that they hang a bamboo full of water over the grave; there is a small hole in the lower end of the bamboo, so that the water drips from it continually. The bamboo is always refilled with water until rain drenches the ground. Here, as in New Caledonia, we find religion blent with magic, for the prayer to the dead chief, which is purely religious, is eked out with a magical imitation of rain at his grave. We have seen that the Baronga of Delagoa Bay drench the tombs of their ancestors, especially the tombs of twins, as a rain-charm. Among some of the Indian tribes in the region of the Orinoco it was customary for the relations of a deceased person to disinter his bones a year after burial, burn them and scatter the ashes to the winds, because they believed that the ashes were changed into rain, which the dead man sent in return for his obsequies. The Chinese are convinced that when human bodies remain unburied, the souls of their late owners feel the discomfort of rain, just as living men would do if they were exposed without shelter to the inclemency of the weather. These wretched souls, therefore, do all in their power to prevent the rain from falling, and often their efforts are only too successful. Then drought ensues, the most dreaded of all calamities in China, because bad harvests, dearth and famine follow in its train. Hence it has been a common practice of the Chinese authorities in time of drought to inter the dry bones of the unburied dead for the purpose of putting an end to the scourge and conjuring down the rain.

176.

The knowledge not of sorrow, you were
        saying, but of boredom
Is—aside from reading speaking
        smoking—
Of what, Maude Blessingbourne it was,
        wished to know when, having risen,
'approached the window as if to see
        what really was going on';
And saw rain falling, in the distance
        more slowly,
The road clear from her past the window-
        glass—
Of the world, weather-swept, with which
        one shares the century.

177.

'That warm April rain. Seven years now I've thought about that rain. The raindrops rolled up like quicksilver. They say that radiation is colourless, but the puddles that day were green and bright yellow ...'

178.

It is a commonplace of conversation that for some months past the weather conditions have been abnormal, particularly in the matter of rainfall, in the battle-zones and elsewhere. Detailed data from regions close to the firing lines are not available; and we have only general statements of inclemency in so far as they affect military operations. But in districts not far away – the British Isles, for instance – the records of excessive raininess during the winter of 1914–15 and at subsequent times have not escaped comment; and others besides meteorologists are discussing the possibility of a connection between the heavy cannonading and the rainfall. The professional meteorologist is called upon to answer whether there is any rational explanation of what appears to be a marked departure from the usual sequence of weather conditions. Is it possible that the tremendous expenditure of ammunition – an expenditure which the layman may well regard as an experiment in concussion sufficiently vast to be decisive – has facilitated condensation and its later stage, precipitation? In concise terms, has the bombarding not only caused clouds but forced the clouds to send down rain?

179.

Rain, midnight rain, nothing but the wild rain
On this bleak hut, and solitude, and me
Remembering again that I shall die
And neither hear the rain nor give it thanks
For washing me cleaner than I have been
Since I was born into this solitude.
Blessed are the dead that the rain rains upon:
But here I pray that none whom once I loved
Is dying tonight or lying still awake

Solitary, listening to the rain,
Either in pain or thus in sympathy
Helpless among the living and the dead,
Like a cold water among broken reeds,
Myriads of broken reeds all still and stiff,
Like me who have no love which this wild rain
Has not dissolved except the love of death,
If love it be towards what is perfect and
Cannot, the tempest tells me, disappoint.

180.

An affable Irregular,
A heavily-built Falstaffian man,
Comes cracking jokes of civil war
As though to die by gunshot were
The finest play under the sun.

A brown Lieutenant and his men,
Half dressed in national uniform,
Stand at my door, and I complain
Of the foul weather, hail and rain,
A pear tree broken by the storm.

I count those feathered balls of soot
The moor-hen guides upon the stream,
To silence the envy in my thought;
And turn towards my chamber, caught
In the cold snows of a dream.

181.

By the North Gate, the wind blows full of sand,
Lonely from the beginning of time until now!
Trees fall, the grass goes yellow with autumn.
I climb the towers and towers
              to watch out the barbarous land:

Desolate castle, the sky, the wide desert.
There is no wall left to this village.
Bones white with a thousand frosts,
High heaps, covered with trees and grass;
Who brought this to pass?
Who has brought the flaming imperial anger?
Who has brought the army with drums and with kettle-drums?
Barbarous kings.
A gracious spring, turned to blood-ravenous autumn,
A turmoil of wars-men, spread over the middle kingdom,
Three hundred and sixty thousand,
And sorrow, sorrow like rain.
Sorrow to go, and sorrow, sorrow returning.
Desolate, desolate fields,
And no children of warfare upon them,
                    No longer the men for offence and defence.
Ah, how shall you know the dreary sorrow at the North Gate,
With Riboku's name forgotten,
And we guardsmen fed to the tigers.

182.

No soldiers in the scenery,
No thoughts of people now dead,
As they were fifty years ago:
Young and living in a live air,
Young and walking in the sunshine,
Bending in blue dresses to touch something –
Today the mind is not part of the weather.

Today the air is clear of everything.
It has no knowledge except of nothingness
And it flows over us without meanings,
As if none of us had ever been here before
And are not now: in this shallow spectacle,
This invisible activity, this sense.

183.

At noon in the desert a panting lizard
waited for history, its elbows tense,
watching the curve of a particular road
as if something might happen.

It was looking at something farther off
than people could see, an important scene
acted in stone for little selves
at the flute end of consequences.

There was just a continent without much on it
under a sky that never cared less.
Ready for a change, the elbows waited.
The hands gripped hard on the desert.

184.

In summers heate and mid-time of the day
To rest my limbes upon a bed I lay,
One window shut, the other open stood,
Which gave such light as twinkles in a wood,
Like twilight glimpse at setting of the Sunne
Or night being past, and yet not day begunne.
Such light to shamefast maidens must be showne,
Where they may sport, and seeme to bee unknowne.
Then came Corinna in a long loose gowne,
Her white neck hid with tresses hanging downe:
Resembling fayre Semiramis going to bed
Or Laïs of a thousand wooers sped.
I snatcht her gowne, being thin, the harme was small,
Yet striv'd she to be covered there withall.
And striving thus as one that would be cast,
Betray'd her selfe, and yielded at the last.
Starke naked as she stood before mine eye,
Not one wen in her body could I spie.

What arms and shoulders did I touch and see,
How apt her breasts were to be prest by me?
How smooth a belly under her waist saw I?
How large a legge, and what a lustie thigh?
To leave the rest, all like'd me passing well,
I cling'd her naked body, downe she fell,
Judge you the rest: being tired she bad me kisse,
Jove send me more such after-noones as this.

185.

But ere he on his journey went, he made his faithful make
Alcyone privy to the thing. Immediately there strake
A chillness to her very bones, and pale was all her face
Like box, and down her heavy cheeks the tears did gush apace.
Three times about to speak, three times she washed her face with
     tears,
And stinting oft with sobs, she thus complainèd in his ears:
'What fault of mine, O husband dear, hath turned thy heart from me?
Where is that care of me that erst was wont to be in thee?
And canst thou having left thy dear Alcyone merry be?
Do journeys long delight thee now? Doth now mine absence please
Thee better than my presence doth? Think I that thou at ease
Shalt go by land? Shall I have cause but only for to mourn
And not to be afraid? And shall my care of thy return
Be void of fear? No no. The sea me sore afraid doth make.
To think upon the sea doth cause my flesh for fear to quake.
I saw the broken ribs of ships alate upon the shore;
And oft on tombs I read their names whose bodies long before
The sea had swallowed.
                              Let not fond vain hope seduce thy mind,
That Aeolus is thy father-in-law who holds the boistrous wind
In prison and can calm the seas at pleasure. When the winds
Are once let loose upon the sea, no order then them binds.
Then neither land hath priviledge, nor sea exemption finds.
Yea, even the clouds of heaven they vex and with their meeting stout
Enforce the fire with hideous noise to brust in flashes out.
The more that I do know them (for right well I know their power

And saw them oft, a little wench within my father's bower)
So much the more I think them to be feared. But if thy will
By no entreatance may be turned at home to tarry still
But that thou needs wilt go: then me, dear husband, with thee take.
So shall the sea us equally together toss and shake:
So worser than I feel I shall be certain not to fear:
So shall we whatsoever haps together jointly bear:
So shall we on the broad main sea together jointly sail.'
These words and tears wherewith the imp of Aeolus did assail
Her husband born of heavenly race, did make his heart relent
For he loved her no less than she loved him. But fully bent
He seemèd, neither for to leave the journey which he meant
To take by sea, nor yet to give Alcyone leave as tho
Companion of his perilous course by water for to go.
He many words of comfort spake her fear away to chase,
But nought he could persuade therein to make her like the case.
This last assuagement of her grief he added in the end,
Which was the only thing that made her loving heart to bend:
'All tarriance will assuredly seem overlong to me.
And by my father's blasing beams I make my vow to thee,
That at the furthest ere the time (if God thereto agree)
The moon do fill her circle twice, again I will here be.'
        When in some hope of his return this promise had her set,
He willed a ship immediately from harbour to be fet,
And throughly riggèd for to be, that neither mast, nor sail,
Nor tackling, no, nor other thing should appertaining fail.
Which when Alcyone did behold, as one whose heart misgave
The haps at hand, she quaked again and tears out gushing drave.
And, straining Ceyx in her arms with pale and piteous look,
Poor wretched soul, her last farewell at length she sadly took,
And swounded flat upon the ground. Anon the watermen
(As Ceyx sought delays and was in doubt to turn again)
Set hand to oars, of which there were two rows on either side,
And all at once with equal stroke the swelling sea divide.
        She lifting up her watery eyes beheld her husband stand
Upon the hatches, making signs by beckoning with his hand;
And she made signs to him again. And after that the land
Was far removèd from the ship, and that the sight began

To be unable to discern the face of any man,
As long as e'er she could, she looked upon the rowing keel.
And when she could no longer time for distance ken it well,
She lookèd still upon the sails that flaskèd with the wind
Upon the mast. And when she could the sails no longer find
She gat her to her empty bed with sad and sorry heart
And laid her down. The chamber did renew afresh her smart
And of her bed did bring to mind the dear departed part.
From harbour now they quite were gone; and now a pleasant gale
Did blow. The master made his men their oars aside to hale
And hoisèd up the topsail on the highest of the mast,
And clapped on all his other sails, because no wind should waste.
Scarce full t'one half (or, sure, not much above) the ship had run
Upon the sea and every way the land did far them shun,
When toward night the wallowing waves began to waxen white
And eke the heady eastern wind did blow with greater might.
Anon the Master crièd, 'Strike the topsail, let the main
Sheet fly and fardel it to the yard!' Thus spake he, but in vain.
For why, so hideous was the storm upon the sudden braid,
That not a man was able there to hear what other said.
And loud the sea with meeting waves extremely raging roars.
Yet fell they to it of themselves. Some haled aside the oars;
Some fencèd in the galley's sides, some down the sailcloths rend;
Some pump the water out and sea to sea again do send;
Another hales the sailyards down. And while they did each thing
Disorderly, the storm increased, and from each quarter fling
The winds with deadly feud and bounce the raging waves together.
The Pilot, being sore dismayed, saith plain, he knows not whither
To wend himself nor what to do or bid, nor in what state
Things stood; so huge the mischief was and did so overmate
All art. For why of rattling ropes, of crying men and boys,
Of flushing waves and thundring air, confusèd was the noise.
The surges, mounting up aloft, did seem to mate the sky
And with their sprinkling for to wet the clouds that hang on high.
One while the sea, when from the brink it raised the yellow sand,
Was like in colour to the same. Another while did stand
A colour on it blacker than the Lake of Styx. Anon
It lieth plain and loometh white with seething froth thereon.

And with the sea the Trachine ship aye alteration took:
One while as from a mountain's top it seemèd down to look
To valleys and the depth of hell; another while, beset
With swelling surges round about which near above it met,
It lookèd from the bottom of the whirlpool up aloft
As if it were from hell to heaven. A hideous flushing oft
The waves did make in beating full against the galley's side.
The galley, being stricken, gave as great a sound that tide
As did sometime the battle-ram of steel or now the gun
In making battery to a tower. And as fierce lions run
Full breast with all their force against the armèd men that stand
In order bent to keep them off with weapons in their hand,
Even so, as often as the waves by force of wind did rave,
So oft upon the netting of the shippe they mainly drave,
And mounted far above the same. Anon off fell the hoopes;
And having washed the pitch away, the sea made open loops
To let the deadly water in. Behold the clouds did melt,
And showers large came pouring down. The seamen that them felt
Might think that all the heaven had fallen upon them that same time
And that the swelling sea likewise above the heaven would climb.
The sails were throughly wet with showers, and with the heavenly rain
Was mixed the waters of the sea. No lights at all remain
Of sun or moon or stars in heaven; the darkness of the night,
Augmented with the dreadful storm, takes double power and might.
Howbeit, the flashing lightnings oft do put the same to flight
And with their glancing now and then do give a sudden light.
The lightning sets the waves on fire. Above the netting skip
The waves and with a violent force do light within the ship.
And as a soldier stouter than the rest of all his band
That oft assails a city walls defended well by hand
At length attains his hope, and, for to purchase praise withall,
Alone among a thousand men gets up upon the wall:
So, when the lofty waves had long the galley's sides assayed,
At length the tenth wave, rising up with huger force and braid,
Did never cease assaulting of the weary ship till that
Upon the hatches like a foe victoriously it gat.
A part thereof did still as yet assault the ship without,
And part had gotten in. The men, all trembling, ran about

As in a city comes to pass when of the enemies some
Dig down the walls without and some already in are come.
All art and cunning was to seek; their hearts and stomachs fail:
And look how many surges came their vessel to assail,
So many deaths did seem to charge and break upon them all.
One weeps: another stands amazed: the third them blest doth call
Whom burial doth remain. To God another makes his vow
And, holding up his hands to heaven, the which he sees not now,
Doth pray in vain for help. The thought of this man is upon
His brother and his parents whom he clearly hath forgone;
Another calls his house and wife and children unto mind,
And every man in general the things he left behynd.
Alcyone moveth Ceyx's heart. In Ceyx's mouth is none
But onely one Alcyone. And though she were alone
The wight that he desirèd most, yet was he very glad
She was not there. To Trachinward to look desire he had,
And homeward fain he would have turned his eyes which never more
Should see the land. But when he knew not which way was the shore,
Nor where he was, the raging sea did roll about so fast
And all the heaven with clouds as black as pitch was overcast
That never night was half so dark, there came a flaw at last
That with his violence brake the mast and strake the stern away.
A billow, proudly pranking up as vaunting of his prey
By conquest gotten, walloweth whole and breaketh not asunder,
Beholding with a lofty look the waters working under.
And look, as if a man should from the places where they grow
Rend down the mountains Athe and Pind, and whole them overthrow
Into the open sea, so soft the billow, tumbling down,
With weight and violent stroke did sink and in the bottom drown
The galley. And the most of them that were within the same
Went downe therewith and never up to open aier came
But dièd strangled in the gulf. Another sort again
Caught pieces of the broken ship. The king himself was fain
A shiver of the sunken ship in that same hand to hold
In which he erst a royal mace had held of yellow gold.
His father and his father-in-law he calls upon (alas
In vain). But chiefly in his mouth his wife Alcyone was.
In heart was shee: in tongue was shee: he wishèd that his corse

To land where she might take it up the surges might enforce,
And that by her most loving hands he might be laid in grave.
In swimming still (as often as the surges leave him gave
To ope his lips) he harped still upon Alcyone's name,
And when he drownèd in the waves he muttered still the same.
Behold, even full upon the wave a flake of water black
Did break and underneath the sea the head of Ceyx strake.
That night the lightsome Lucifer for sorrow was so dim
As scarcely could a man discerne or think it to be him.
And for as much as out of heaven he might not step aside,
With thick and darksome clouds that night his count'nance he did hide.
Alcyone, of so great mischaunce not knowing aught as yet,
Did keep a reckoning of the nights that in the while did flit
And hasted garments both for him and for herself likewise
To wear at his homecoming, which she vainly did surmise.
To all the Gods devoutly she did offer frankincense,
But most above them all the church of Juno she did cense.
And for her husband (who as then was none) she kneeled before
The altar, wishing health and soon arrival at the shore
And that none other woman might before her be preferred.
Of all her prayers this one piece effectually was heard.
For Juno could not find in heart entreated for to be
For him that was already dead. But to th'intent that she
From Dame Alcyone's deadly hands might keep her altars free,
She said, 'Most faithful messenger of my commandments, O
Thou rainbow, to the sluggish house of Slumber swiftly go
And bid him send a dream in shape of Ceyx to his wife
Alcyone, for to show her plain the losing of his life.'
Dame Iris takes her pall wherein a thousand colours were,
And, bowing like a stringèd bow upon the cloudy sphere,
Immediately descended to the drowsy house of Sleep
Whose court the clouds continually do closely overdreep.
Among the darke Cimmerians is a hollow mountain found
And in the hill a Cave that far doth run within the ground,
The chamber and the dwelling place where slothful sleep doth couch.
The light of Phoebus' golden beams this place can never touch.
A foggy mist with dimness mixed streams upward from the ground,
And glimmering twilight evermore within the same is found.

No watchful bird with barbèd bill and combèd crown doth call
The morning forth with crowing out. There is no noise at all
Of waking dog nor gaggling goose, more waker than the hound,
To hinder sleep. Of beast ne wild ne tame there is no sound.
No boughs are stirred with blasts of wind, no noise of tattling tongue
Of man or woman ever yet within that bower rung.
Dumb quiet dwelleth there. Yet from the roche's foot doth go
The river of Forgetfulness, which runneth trickling so
Upon the little pebble stones which in the channell lie
That unto sleep a great deal more it doth provoke thereby.
Before the entry of the cave there grows a poppy store
With seeded heads and other weeds innumerable more,
Out of the milky juice of which the night doth gather sleeps
And over all the shadowed earth with dankish dew them dreeps.
Bycause the craking hinges of the doore no noise should make,
There is no door in all the house nor porter at the gate.
Amid the cave, of ebony a bedstead standeth high
And on the same a bed of down with coverings black doth lie
In which the drowsy god of sleep his lither limbs doth rest.
About him, forging sundry shapes, as many dreams lie pressed
As ears of corn do stand in fields in harvest time, or leaves
Do grow on trees, or sea to shore of sandy cinder heaves.
      As soon as Iris came within this house and with her hand
Had put aside the dazzling dreams that in her way did stand,
The brightness of her robe through all the sacred house did shine.
The God of sleep scarce able for to raise his heavy eyen,
A three or four times at the least did fall again to rest
And with his nodding head did knock his chin against his breast.
At length he, shaking of himself, upon his elbow leaned.
And, though he knew for what she came, he asked her what she
    meant.
'O sleepe,' quoth shee, 'the rest of things, O gentlest of the gods,
Sweete sleep, the peace of mind with whom crook'd care is aye at odds,
Which cherishest men's weery limbs appalled with toiling sore
And makest them as fresh to work and lusty as before,
Command a dream (that in their kinds can everything express)
To Trachin, Hercl'es' town, himself this instant to address;
And let him lively counterfeit to Queen Alcyone

The image of her husband who is drownèd in the sea
By shipwreck. Juno willeth so.' Her message being told,
Dame Iris went her way: she could her eyes no longer hold
From sleep. But when she felt it com, she fled that instant time
And by the bow that brought her down to heaven again did climb.
      Among a thousand sons and mo that father Slumber had,
He calld up Morph, the feigner of man's shape, a crafty lad.
None other could so cunningly expresse man's very face,
His gesture and his sound of voice, and manner of his pace,
Together with his wonted weed and wonted phrase of talk.
But this same Morphey only in the shape of man doth walk.
There is another who the shapes of beast or bird doth take
Or else appeareth unto men in likeness of a snake.
The gods do call him Icelos, and mortal folk him name
Phobctor. There is also yet a third who from these same
Works diversely, and Phantasos he highteth; into streams
This turns himself and into stones and earth and timber beams
And into every other thing that wanteth life. These three
Great kings and captains in the night are wonted for to see.
The meaner and inferior sort of others haunted be.
Sir Slumber overpassed the rest, and of the brothers all
To do Dame Iris' message he did only Morphey call.
Which done, he, waxing luskish, straight laid down his drowsy head
And softly shrunk his lazy limbs within his sluggish bed.
Away flew Morphey through the aire – no flickering made his wings –
And came anon to Trachin. There his feathers off he flings
And in the shape of Ceyx stands before Alcyone's bed,
Pale, wan, stark nak'd and like a man that was but lately dead.
His beard seemed wet, and of his head the hair was dropping dry.
And, leaning on her bed, with tears he seemèd thus to cry:
'Most wretched woman, knowest thou thy loving Ceyx now?
Or is my face by death deformed? Behold me well, and thou
Shalt know me. For thy husband, thou thy husband's ghost shalt see.
No good thy prayers and thy vows have done at all to me.
For I am dead. In vain of my return no reckoning make.
The cloudy south amid the sea our ship did tardy take
And, tossing it with violent blasts, asunder did it shake.
And floods have filled my mouth which called in vain upon thy name.

No person whom thou mayst misdeem brings tidings of the same,
Thou hearest not thereof by false report of flying fame,
But I myself. I presently my shipwreck to thee show.
Arise, therefore, and woeful tears upon thy spouse bestow.
Put mourning raiment on, and let me not to Limbo go
Unmourned for.' In showing of this shipwreck, Morphey so
Did feign the voice of Ceyx that she could none other deem
But that it should be his indeed. Moreover he did seem
To weep in earnest: and his hands the very gesture had
Of Ceyx. Queene Alcyone did groan, and, being sad,
Did stir her arms and thrust them forth his body to embrace.
Instead whereof she caught but air. The tears ran down her face.
She cryed, 'Tarry! Whither fly'st? Together let us go!'
And all this while she was asleep. Both with her crying so
And flighted with the image of her husband's gastly sprite
She started up and sought about if find him there she might
(For why her grooms, awaking with the shriek, had brought a light).
And when she nowhere could him find, she gan her face to smite
And tare her nightclothes from her breast and strake it fiercely and,
Not passing to unty her hair, she rent it with her hand.
And when her nurse of this her grief desired to understand
The cause, 'Alcoyne is undone, undone and cast away
With Ceyx, her dear spouse,' she said. 'Leave comforting, I pray.
By shipwreck he is perished; I have seen him; and I knew
His hands. When in departing I to hold him did pursue
I caught a ghost; but such a ghost as well discern I might
To be my husband's. Natheless he had not to my sight
His wonted countenance, neither did his visage shine so bright
As heretofore it had beene wont. I saw him, wretched wight,
Stark naked, pale and with his hair still wet; even very here
I saw him stand.' With that she looks if any print appear
Of footing whereas he did stand upon the floor behind.
'This, this is it that I did fear in far-forecasting mind
When, flying me, I thee desired thou should not trust the wind.
But sith thou wentest to thy death, I would that I had gone
With thee. Ah, meet, it meet had been thou should'st not go alone
Without me. So it should have come to pass that neither I
Had overlivèd thee, nor yet been forcèd twice to die.

Already absent in the waves now tossèd have I be.
Already have I perished. And yet the sea hath thee
Without me. But the cruelness were greater far of me
Than of the sea, if after thy decease I still would strive
In sorrow and in anguish still to pine away alive.
But neither will I strive in care to lengthen still my life,
Nor (wretched wight) abandon thee, but like a faithful wife
At leastwise now will come as thy companion. And the hearse
Shall join us, though not in the selfsame coffin, yet in verse.
Although in tomb the bones of us together may not couch,
Yet in a graven epitaph my name thy name shall touch.'
Her sorrow would not suffer her to utter any more.
She sobbed and sighed at every word until her heart was sore.
The morning came, and out she went right pensive to the shore
To that same place in which she took her leave of him before.
While there she musing stood, and said, 'He kissed me even here,
Here weighèd he his anchors up, here loosed he from the pier.'
And while she called to mind the things there markèd with her eyes,
In looking on the open sea a great way of she spies
A certain thing much like a corse come hovering on the wave.
At first she doubted what it was. As tide it nearer drave,
Although it were a good way off, yet did it plainly show
To be a corse. And though that whose it was she did not know,
Yet for because it seemed a wreck, her heart therat did rise.
And as it had some stranger been, with water in her eyes
She said, 'Alas, poor wretch, whoe'er thou art, alas for her
That is thy wife, if any be.' And as the waves did stir,
The body floated nearer land; the which the more that she
Beheld, the less began in her of staïd wit to be.
Anon it did arrive on shore. Then plainly she did see
And know it, that it was her fere. She shriekèd, 'It is he!'
And therewithal her face, her hair and garments she did tear
And, unto Ceyx stretching out her trembling hands with fear,
Said, Com'st thou home in such a plight to me, O husband dear?
Return'st in such a wretched plight?' There was a certain pier
That builded was by hand of waves the first assaults to break,
And at the haven's mouth to cause the tide to enter weak.
She leapt thereon. (A wonder sure it was she could do so)

She flew and with her new-grown wings did beat the ayre as tho;
And on the waves, a wretched bird, she whiskèd to and fro.
And with her croaking neb, then grown to slender bill and round,
Like one that wailed and mournèd still she made a moaning sound.
Howbeit, as soon as she did touch his dumb and bloodless flesh,
And had embraced his lovèd limbs with wings made new and fresh
And with her hardened neb had kissed him coldly, though in vain,
Folk doubt if Ceyx, feeling it, to raise his head did strain,
Or whether that the waves did lift it up; but surely he
It felt. And through compassion of the gods both he and she
Were turned to birds. The love of them eke subject to their fate
Continued after; neither did the faithful bond abate
Of wedlock in them, being birds, but stands in steadfast state.
They tread and lay and bring forth young, and now the alcyon sitts
In wintertime upon her nest (which on the water flits)
A sevennight, during all which time the sea is calm and still
And every man may to and fro sail safely at his will.
For Aeolus for his offspring's sake the winds at home doth keep
And will not let them go abroad for troubling of the deep.

186.

Our storm is past, and that storm's tyrannous rage,
A stupid calm, but nothing it, doth 'suage.
The fable is inverted, and farre more
A blocke afflicts, now, than a storke before.
Storms chafe, and soon wear out themselves, or us;
In calms, Heaven laughs to see us languish thus.
As steady'as I can wish that my thoughts were,
Smooth as thy mistress' glass, or what shines there,
The sea is now. And, as the Iles which wee
Seeke, when wee can move, our ships rooted bee.
As water did in stormes, now pitch runs out,
As lead, when a fir'd Church becomes one spout.
And all our beauty, and our trimme, decayse,

Like courts removing, or like ended playes.
The fighting-place now seamen's ragges supply;
And all the tackling is a frippery.
No use of lanthornes; and in one place lay
Feathers and dust, today and yesterday.
Earth's hollownesses, which the world's lungs are,
Have no more wind than th'upper vault of aire.
We can nor lost friends, nor sought foes recover,
But meteor-like, save that wee move not, hover.
Only the Calenture together drawes
Deare friends, which meet dead in great fishes' jawes;
And on the hatches, as on Altars, lyes
Each one, his owne Priest, and owne Sacrifice.

187.

When the low, heavy sky weighs like a lid on the spirit as it groans, in
the grip of long tedium; and when, filling the whole circle of the
horizon, it spreads over us a black daylight gloomier than night;

When the earth is changed to a humid dungeon where Hope, like a
bat, flies about beating its mild wings against the walls and knocking
its head on rotten ceilings;

When the rain, dragging out its immense, oblique lines, mimics the
bars of a vast prison, and a silent tribe of filthy spiders starts to spin
its webs in the depths of our brains;

Suddenly church bells leap furiously to life and begin their ghastly
howling at heaven, like wandering homeless spirits whimpering
together unstoppably.

– And long funeral processions, without drums or music, file slowly
past in my soul. Hope, defeated, weeps, and cruel despotic anguish
plants its black flag in my bowed skull.

CURSE

the flabby sky that can manufacture no snow, but can only drop the sea on us in a drizzle like a poem by Mr. Robert Bridges.

CURSE

the lazy air that cannot stiffen the back of the SERPENTINE, or put Aquatic steel half way down the MANCHESTER CANAL.

———

But ten years ago we saw distinctly both snow and ice here.

May some vulgarly inventive, but useful person, arise, and restore us to the necessary BLIZZARDS.

LET US ONCE MORE WEAR THE ERMINE OF THE NORTH.

WE BELIEVE IN THE EXISTENCE OF THIS USEFUL LITTLE CHEMIST IN OUR MIDST !

189.

(The Weather in This Book)

No weather will be found in this book. This is an attempt to pull a book through without weather. It being the first attempt of the kind in fictitious literature, it may prove a failure, but it seemed worth the while of some dare-devil person to try it, and the author was in just the mood.

Many a reader who wanted to read a tale through was not able to do it because of delays on account of the weather. Nothing breaks up an author's progress like having to stop every few pages to fuss-up the weather. Thus it is plain that persistent intrusions of weather are bad for both reader and author.

Of course weather is necessary to a narrative of human experience. That is conceded. But it ought to be put where it will not be in the way; where it will not interrupt the flow of the narrative. And it ought to be the ablest weather that can be had, not ignorant, poor-quality, amateur weather. Weather is a literary specialty, and no untrained hand can turn out a good article of it. The present author can do only a few trifling ordinary kinds of weather, and he cannot do those very good. So it has seemed wisest to borrow such weather as is necessary for the book from qualified and recognized experts—giving credit, of course. This weather will be found over in the back part of the book, out of the way. See Appendix. The reader is requested to turn over and help himself from time to time as he goes along.

190.

SIR NICHOLAS GIMCRACK.   By the way, Gentlemen, what Countrey air do you like best?
BRUCE.   Why we cannot travel far for't this evening.
SIR NICHOLAS.   Travel! I thought I should have you. Why I never travel, I take it in a close chamber.
BRUCE.   Why, you can take but one kind of nasty smoaky air in a Chamber.
SIR NICHOLAS.   There's your Mistake. Chuse your Air, you shall have it in my Chamber; *Newmarket, Banstead-down, Wiltshire, Bury*-air, *Norwich*-air; what you will.

BRUCE.   Would a man think it possible for a Virtuoso to arrive at this extravagance?
LONGVIL.   Yes, I assure you; it is beyond the wit of man to invent such extravagant things for them, as their folly finds out for themselves. Is it possible to take all these several Countrey Airs in your Chamber?
SIR NICHOLAS.   I knew you were to seek. I employ men all over *England*, Factors for Air, who bottle up Air, and weigh it in all places, sealing the Bottles Hermetically: they send me Loads from all places. That Vault is full of Countrey-air.
BRUCE.   To weigh Air, and send it to you!
SIR NICHOLAS.   O yes, I have sent one to weigh Air at the Picque of *Teneriff*, that's the lightest Air. I shall have a considerable Cargo of that Air. *Sheerness* and the *Isle of Dogs* Air is the heaviest. Now if I have a mind to take Countrey Air, I send for, may be, forty Gallons of *Bury* Air, shut all my windows and doors close, and let it fly in my Chamber.
BRUCE.   This is a most admirable invention.
LONGVIL.   But to what purpose do you weigh Air?
SIR NICHOLAS.   That I shall tell you as we are taking it.

191.

Experimental physics has succeeded, during the last decade of the century, in reducing all gaseous bodies to a liquid – most of them, also, to a solid – condition. Nothing more is needed than special apparatus, which exerts a violent pressure on the gases at a very low temperature … With this transformation the mystic nimbus which formerly veiled the character of the gas in popular estimation – as an invisible body that wrought visible effects – has entirely disappeared. If, then, the substance of the soul were really gaseous, it should be possible to liquefy it by the application of a high pressure at a low temperature. We could then catch the soul as it is 'breathed out' at the moment of death, condense it, and exhibit it in a bottle as 'immortal fluid' (*Fluidum animae immortale*). By a further lowering of temperature and increase of pressure it might be possible to solidify it – to produce '*soul-snow*'. The experiment has not yet succeeded.

192.

Westron wynde when wyll thou blow,
The smalle rayne downe can rayne –
Cryst, yf my love wer in my armys
And I yn my bed agayne!

193.

In Titane there is also a sanctuary of Athena, to which they carry up
Coronis: it contains an ancient wooden idol of Athena, which is also
said to have been struck by lightning. After descending from this hill
(for the sanctuary is built on a hill) we come to an altar of the winds,
on which the priest sacrifices to the winds one night in every year. He
also performs other secret rites at four pits, taming the fury of the
blasts; and he chants, they say, Medea's spells.

194.

Now the Sun, the rain, the shine, the thunder, they are alive. But they
are not persons or people. They are alive. They are manifestations of
living activity. But they are not personal Gods.

Everything lives. Thunder lives, and rain lives, and sunshine lives.
But not in the personal sense.

How is man to get himself into relation with the vast living
convulsions of rain and thunder and sun, which are conscious and
alive and potent, but like vastest of beasts, inscrutable and
incomprehensible. How is man to get himself into relation with these,
the vastest of cosmic beasts? (…)

The American-Indian sees no division into Spirit and Matter, God
and Not-God. Everything is alive, though not personally so. Thunder
is neither Thor nor Zeus. Thunder is the vast living thunder asserting
itself like some incomprehensible monster, or some huge reptile-bird
of the pristine cosmos.

How to conquer the dragon-mouthed thunder! How to capture
the feathered rain!

195.

'Hear, Imlac, what thou wilt not without difficulty credit. I have
possessed for five years the regulation of the weather, and the
distribution of the seasons: the sun has listened to my dictates, and
passed from tropick to tropick by my direction; the clouds, at my call,
have poured their waters, and the Nile has overflowed at my
command; I have restrained the rage of the dog-star, and mitigated
the fervours of the crab. The winds alone, of all the elemental powers,
have hitherto refused my authority, and multitudes have perished by
equinoctial tempests which I found myself unable to prohibit or
restrain. I have administered this great office with exact justice, and
made to the different nations of the earth an impartial dividend of
rain and sunshine. What must have been the misery of half the globe,
if I had limited the clouds to particular regions, or confined the sun
to either side of the equator? (…)

'I have diligently considered the position of the earth and sun, and
formed innumerable schemes in which I changed their situation. I
have sometimes turned aside the axis of the earth, and sometimes
varied the ecliptick of the sun: but I have found it impossible to make
a disposition by which the world may be advantaged; what one region
gains, another loses by an imaginable alteration, even without
considering the distant parts of the solar system with which we are
unacquainted. Do not, therefore, in thy administration of the year,
indulge thy pride by innovation; do not please thyself with thinking
that thou canst make thyself renowned to all future ages, by
disordering the seasons. The memory of mischief is no desirable
fame. Much less will it become thee to let kindness or interest
prevail. Never rob other countries of rain to pour it on thine own.
For us the Nile is sufficient.'

196.

… War broke out between the Lydians and the Medes, and lasted for
five years, during which sometimes the Medes won and sometimes
the Lydians; there was also one battle by night. The war was proving
to be an equal contest, and in the sixth year it happened that, when

the fight had begun, and the combatants were already closely
engaged, suddenly day became night. The occurrence of this eclipse
had already been predicted to the Ionians by Thales the Milesian, for
which he had set a date in this very year. The Lydians and the Medes,
however, when they saw night instead of day, ceased from fighting,
and both were suddenly more eager to make peace.

197.

Light of the sun, what have you contrived, far-seeing one,
O mother of eyesight, supreme star,
by being hidden in daytime? A rushing road of darkness
rolled out in place of day,
why have you confounded
men's strength and wisdom's way?
Is it to bring some unprecedented disaster?
But I beseech you, swift driver of horses, in the name of Zeus
turn this universal omen, O Lady,
into some harmless blessing for Thebes.

Do you bring the portent of some war,
or the failure of crops, or a mighty snowstorm
beyond telling, or murderous civil war,
or the sea emptying over the plain,
or freezing of the earth, or a wet summer
flowing with raging rain,
or will you flood the land and make
a new race of men from the beginning?

198.

GLOUCESTER. These late Eclipses in the Sun and Moone portend
no good to us: though the wisedome of Nature can reason it thus, and
thus, yet Nature finds itselfe scourg'd by the sequent effects. Love
cooles, friendship falls off, Brothers divide. In Cities, mutinies; in
Countries, discord; in Pallaces, Treason; and the Bond crack'd, 'twixt

Sonne and Father. This villaine of mine comes under the prediction; there's Son against Father, the King falls from bias of Nature; there's Father against Childe. We have seen the best of our time. Machinations, hollowness, treacherie, and all ruinous disorders follow us disquietly to our Graves ...   (*Exit*)

EDMUND.   This is the excellent foppery of the world, that, when we are sicke in fortune, often the surfeit of our own behavior, we make guilty of our disasters the Sun, the Moone, and the Starres: as if we were villaines by necessitie, Fooles by heavenly compulsion; Knaves, Theeves and Treachers by Sphericall predominance; Drunkards, Lyars, and Adulterers by an inforc'd obedience of Planetary influence; and all that we are evill in, by a divine thrusting on. An admirable evasion of Whore-master-man, to lay his Goatish disposition to the charge of a Starre. My father compounded with my mother under the Dragon's taile, and my Nativity was under *Ursa Major*, so that it followes, I am rough and Lecherous. I should have bin that I am, had the maidenlest Starre in the Firmament twinkled on my bastardizing.

199.

It happen'd once, that a Discourse began between the Father and Mother about the Eclipse of the Sun, which fell out in April 22. 1715. The Eclipse of the Sun was the Subject of all Conversation at that time, having been, as is well known, so Total, and the Darkness so great, as that the like had not been known in that Age, or some hundreds of Years before

The Wife had enquired of her Husband, what the Nature of the Thing was, and he was describing it to her and the Children in a familiar way; and, as I said, that a kind of Reflection upon one another was the usual Issue of their common Discourse, so it was there; the Husband tells her, that the Moon was like a cross Wife, that when she was out of Humour, could Thwart and Eclipse her Husband whenever she pleased; and that if an ill Wife stood in the Way, the brightest Husband could not shine.

She flew in a Passion at this, and being of a sharp Wit, 'you do well, says she, to carry your Emblem to a suitable height; I warrant, you think a Wife, like the Moon, has no Light but what she borrows from her Husband, and that we can only shine by Reflection; it is necessary then you should know, she can Eclipse him when she pleases.'

'Ay, ay,' says the Husband, 'but you see when she does, she darkens the whole House, she can give no Light without him.'

(Upon this she came closer to him:)

WIFE.   I suppose you think you have been Eclips'd lately, we don't see the House is the darker for it.

HUSBAND.   That's because of your own Darkness; I think the House has been much the darker.

WIFE.   None of the Family are made sensible of it, we don't miss your Light.

HUSBAND.   It's strange if they don't, for I see no Light you give in the room of it.

WIFE.   We are but as dark as we were before; for we were none of us the better for all your Hypocritical Shining.

HUSBAND.   Well, I have done shining, you see; the Darkness be at your Door.

(It is evident that both refer to his having left off Family-Worship; and it is apparent, both were come to a dreadful Extremity in their Quarrel.)

WIFE.   At my Door! am I the Master of the Family! don't lay your Sins to my Charge.

HUSBAND.   No, no; but your own I may; It is the Retrograde Motion of the Moon that causes an Eclipse.

WIFE.   Where all was dark before, there can be no Eclipse.

HUSBAND.   Your Sin is, that my Light is your Darkness.

200.

Nothing in the world is astonishing,
unbelievable or forsworn anymore,
now that Zeus has made night out of noon
and hidden away the blazing light of the sun:
wet fear comes upon men.

201.

Lana Turner has collapsed!
I was trotting along and suddenly
it started raining and snowing
and you said it was hailing
but hailing hits you on the head
hard so it was really snowing and
raining and I was in such a hurry
to meet you but the traffic
was acting exactly like the sky
and suddenly I see a headline
LANA TURNER HAS COLLAPSED!
there is no snow in Hollywood
there is no rain in California
I have been to lots of parties
and acted perfectly disgraceful
but I never actually collapsed
oh Lana Turner we love you get up

202.

Somewhere nowhere in Utah, a boy by the roadside,
gun in his hand, and the rare dumb hard tears flowing.
Beside him, a greyheaded man has let one arm slide
awkwardly over his shoulders, is talking and pointing
at whatever it is, dead, in the dust on the ground.

By the old parked Chevy, two women, talking and watching.
Their skirts flag forward, bandanna twist with their hair.
Around them, sheep and a fence and the sagebrush burning
and burning with a blue flame. In the distance, where
mountains are clouds, lightning, but no rain.

203.

There is something uneasy in the Los Angeles air this afternoon,
some unnatural stillness, some tension. What it means is that tonight
a Santa Ana will begin to blow, a hot wind from the northeast

whining down through the Cajon and San Gorgonio Passes, blowing up sand storms out along Route 66, drying the hills and the nerves to flash point. For a few days now we will see smoke back in the canyons, and hear sirens in the night.

I have neither heard nor read that a Santa Ana is due, but I know it, and almost everyone I have seen today knows it too. We know it because we feel it. The baby frets. The maid sulks. I rekindle a waning argument with the telephone company, then cut my losses and lie down, given over to whatever it is in the air. To live with the Santa Ana is to accept, consciously or unconsciously, a deeply mechanistic view of human behavior.

I recall being told, when I first moved to Los Angeles and was living on an isolated beach, that the Indians would throw themselves into the sea when the bad wind blew. I could see why. The Pacific turned ominously glossy during a Santa Ana period, and one woke in the night troubled not only by the peacocks screaming in the olive trees but by the eerie absence of surf. The heat was surreal. The sky had a yellow cast, the kind of light sometimes called 'earthquake weather.' My only neighbor would not come out of her house for days, and there were no lights at night, and her husband roamed the place with a machete. One day he would tell me that he had heard a trespasser, the next a rattlesnake.

'On nights like that,' Raymond Chandler once wrote about the Santa Ana, 'every booze party ends in a fight. Meek little wives feel the edge of the carving knife and study their husbands' necks. Anything can happen.' That was the kind of wind it was. I did not know then that there was any basis for the effect it had on all of us, but it turns out to be another of those cases in which science bears out folk wisdom.

The Santa Ana, which is named for one of the canyons it rushes through, is *foehn* wind, like the *foehn* of Austria and Switzerland and the *hamsin* of Israel. There are a number of persistent malevolent winds, perhaps the best know of which are the mistral of France and the Mediterranean sirocco, but a *foehn* wind has distinct characteristics: it occurs on the leeward slope of a mountain range and, although the air begins as a cold mass, it is warmed as it comes down the mountain and appears finally as a hot dry wind. Whenever and wherever *foehn* blows, doctors hear about headaches and nausea and allergies, about 'nervousness,' about 'depression.'

In Los Angeles some teachers do not attempt to conduct formal classes during a Santa Ana, because the children become unmanageable. In Switzerland the suicide rate goes up during the *foehn*, and in the courts of some Swiss cantons the wind is considered a mitigating circumstance for crime. Surgeons are said to watch the wind, because blood does not clot normally during a *foehn*.

A few years ago an Israeli physicist discovered that not only during such winds, but for the ten or twelve hours which precede them, the air carries an unusually high ratio of positive to negative ions. No one seems to know exactly why that should be; some talk about friction and others suggest solar disturbances. In any case the positive ions are there, and what an excess of positive ions does, in the simplest terms, is make people unhappy. One cannot get much more mechanistic than that.

204.

What more there is lies within the mountain. Something moves between me and it. Place and a mind may interpenetrate till the nature of both is altered. I cannot tell what this movement is except by recounting it.

205.

… I will at present only mention that the sun has for years spoken with me in human words and thereby reveals herself as a living being, or as the organ of a still higher being behind her. God also regulates the weather; as a rule this is done automatically, so to speak, by the greater or lesser amount of heat emanating from the sun, but He can also regulate it in certain ways in pursuit of His own purposes. For instance I have received fairly definite indications that the severe winter of 1870–71 was decided by God in order to turn the fortunes of war in favour of the Germans; and the proud words on the destruction of Philip II's Spanish Armada in the year 1588 *Deus afflavit et dissipati sunt* (God blew the wind and they were scattered) most probably also contain a historical truth. In this connection I refer to the sun only as the instrument of God's willpower which lies nearest to the earth; in reality the condition of the weather is affected by the sum total of the other stars as well. Winds or storms in particular arise when God moves further away from the earth. In circumstances contrary to the Order of the World which have now arisen, this relation has changed – and I wish to mention this at the outset – the weather is now to a certain extent dependent on *my* actions and thoughts; as soon as I indulge in thinking nothing, or in other words cease performing an activity which proves the existence of the human mind, such as playing chess in the garden, the winds arise at once.

206.

ULYSSES.   As soon as her shed blood reddened the earth, the gods thundered audibly above the altar. The wind shivered the air with excited whispering and the sea answered by bellowing. The far shore roared and went white with foam and the funeral flame lit itself. Then the sky flickered with lightning and cracked open and threw down a holy horror to reassure us. The shocked soldier said that Diana descended in a cloud directly into the fire and he thought that she carried our vows and our incense right through the flames to heaven.

207.

Eros shook my
mind like a mountain wind falling on oak trees

208.

But the winds go to every tree, fingering every leaf and branch and furrowed bole; not one is forgotten; the Mountain Pine towering with outstretched arms on the rugged buttresses of the icy peaks, the lowliest and most retiring tenant of the dells; they seek and find them all, caressing them tenderly, bending them in lusty exercise, stimulating their growth, plucking off a leaf or limb as required, or removing an entire tree or grove, now whispering and cooing through the branches like a sleepy child, now roaring like the ocean;

the winds blessing the forests, the forests the winds, with ineffable beauty and harmony as the sure result.

After one has seen pines six feet in diameter bending like grasses before a mountain gale, and ever and anon some giant falling with a crash that shakes the hills, it seems astonishing that any, save the lowest thickset trees, could ever have found a period sufficiently stormless to establish themselves; or, once established, that they should not, sooner or later, have been blown down. But when the storm is over, and we behold the same forests tranquil again, towering fresh and unscathed in erect majesty, and consider what centuries of storms have fallen upon them since they were first planted – hail, to break the tender seedlings; lightning, to scorch and shatter; snow, winds, and avalanches, to crush and overwhelm – while the manifest result of all this wild storm-culture is the glorious perfection we behold; then faith in Nature's forestry is established, and we cease to deplore the violence of her most destructive gales, or of any other storm-implement whatsoever.

There are two trees in the Sierra forests that are never blown down, so long as they continue in sound health. These are the Juniper and the Dwarf Pine of the summit peaks. Their stiff, crooked roots grip the storm-beaten ledges like eagles' claws, while their lithe, cord-like branches bend round compliantly, offering but slight holds for winds, however violent.

209.

There's teuch sauchs growin' i' the Reuch Heuch Hauch.
Like the sauls o' the damned are they,
And ilk ane yoked in a whirligig
Is birlin' the lee-lang day.

O we come doon frae oor stormiest moods,
And licht like a bird i' the haun',
But the teuch sauchs there i' the Reuch Heuch Hauch
As the deil's ain hert are thrawn.

The winds 'ud pu' them up by the roots,
Tho' it broke the warl' asunder,

But they rin richt doon thro' the boddom o' Hell,
And nane kens hoo fer under!

There's no' a licht that the Heavens let loose
Can calm them a hanlawhile,
Nor frae their ancient amplefeyst
Sall God's ain sel' them wile.

210.

It must be remembered, that while our language is yet living, and
variable by the caprice of every one that speaks it, these words are
hourly shifting their relations, and can no more be ascertained in a
dictionary, than a grove, in the agitation of a storm, can be accurately
delineated from its picture in the water.

211.

This is the wind, the wind in a field of corn.
Great crowds are fleeing from a major disaster
Down the long valleys, the green swaying wadis,
Down through the beautiful catastrophe of wind.

Families, tribes, nations, and their livestock
Have heard something, seen something. An expectation
Or a gigantic misunderstanding has swept over the hilltop
Bending the ear of the hedgerow with stories of fire and sword.

I saw a thousand years pass in two seconds.
Land was lost, languages rose and divided.
This lord went east and found safety.
His brother sought Africa and a dish of aloes.

Centuries, minutes later, one might ask
How the hilt of a sword wandered so far from the smithy.
And somewhere they will sing: 'Like chaff we were borne
In the wind.' This is the wind in a field of corn.

212.

I left the spot,
And reascending the bare slope I saw
A naked pool that lay beneath the hills,
The beacon on the summit, and more near
A girl who bore a pitcher on her head
And seemed with difficult steps to force her way
Against the blowing wind. It was in truth
An ordinary sight, but I should need
Colours and words that are unknown to man
To paint the visionary dreariness
Which, while I looked all round for my lost guide,
Did at that time invest the naked pool,
The beacon on the lonely eminence,
The woman and her garments vexed and tossed
By the strong wind.

213.

1. Describe the winds according to the method observed at sea, and give them names either ancient or modern; but let them be constant and invariable.

2. Winds are either General, Periodical, Attendant, or Free. By the General winds, I mean those which blow always; by the Periodical, I mean those which blow at certain times; by the Attendant, those which blow more frequently; and by the Free, those which blow indifferently.

3. What winds are annual, or periodical, and in what countries ? Is any wind so precisely periodical as to return regularly on certain days and hours like the tide of the sea?

4. What winds are attendant and haunters of particular Attendant regions? at what times do they blow in those regions? what winds blow in the spring, summer, autumn, and winter? which are equinoctial, and which solatitial winds? which are morning, which noonday, which evening, and which night winds? (…)

7. The local origins of winds are three in number; for they are either sent down from above, or they spring out of the earth, or they are collected in the body of the air.

8. The generations of the winds are not only original, but also accidental; that is, arising from the compressions, percussion, and repercussions of the air.

9. So much then for the community of winds. But there are some extraordinary and prodigious winds, as fiery winds, whirl-winds, and hurricanes. These prevail on earth. But there are likewise subterranean winds, whereof some are vaporous and mercurial; as are felt in mines; others are sulphureous; and find vent in earthquakes, or burst out from volcanoes.

10. Inquire into these extraordinary and prodigious Winds, and into all the wonderful properties of winds.

11. Of astrological considerations touching the winds inquire sparingly, neither care thou for the over curious schemes of the heaven; only do not neglect the more evident manifest observations of the winds increasing at the rising of certain stars, at the eclipses of luminaries, or at the conjunctions of planets; and how far they depend on the paths of the sun or moon.

12. What do meteors of different kinds contribute to the winds? What do earthquakes, showers, and the meeting of the winds together, contribute? For these things are linked together, and depend one upon the other.

13. What do different vapours and exhalations contribute? which of them is most productive of winds, and how far is the nature of winds influenced by their matter?

14. What do earthly things and things which take place on earth contribute to the winds? What do mountains and the melting of snow upon them, or vast icebergs which float and are borne about in the sea everywhere, contribute? What do the differences of soil or land (if in large tracts), as marshes, sands, woods, plains, contribute? What

the work done by the hand of man, as the burnings of heath and the like for the cultivation of land; the burnings of corn and villages in wars; the draining of marshes; the perpetual discharges of cannon; and the ringing of bells in great cities? Such matters indeed appear trivial, but yet they have some influence.

15. Inquire into all the methods of exciting or calming the winds, but less fully into such as are fabulous or superstitious.

16. Inquire carefully into the height or elevation of the the limits of winds, and if there be any mountain tops where they do not blow; or if the clouds sometimes appear motionless and stationary, at the same time that the winds are blowing strong on the earth. (...)

18. From the limits of the winds let the inquiry pass on to their successions, either among themselves, or with respect to rain and showers. For as they perform a dance, it would be pleasant to know the order of it.

214.

(*Song on applying war paint*)

At the centre of the earth
I stand,
behold me!
At the wind centre
I stand,
Behold me!
A root of herb (medicine)
therefore
I stand,
at the wind centre
I stand.

215.

1. Once the walls have been raised, and the town fortified, the next step is the division into lots of the area contained within the walls, and the orientation of streets and alleys. They will be properly laid out if foresight is employed to prevent the alleys from facing into the pathe of the prevailing winds. Cold winds are disagreeable, hot winds corrupt, moist winds are noxious. It is self-evident that the alignment of streets and side streets ought to follow the angles between the regions of two different winds. (...)

5. Some have held that there are only four winds: Solanus from due east; Auster from the south; Favonius from due west; Septentrio from the north. But more careful investigators tell us that there are eight winds. To find the directions and quarters of the winds, your method of procedure should be as follows.

6. In the middle of the city place a marble *amussium* (horizontal wheel for denoting the direction of the wind), laying it true by the level, or else let the spot be made so true by means of rule and level that no *amussium* is necessary. In the very centre of that spot set up a bronze gnomon or 'shadow tracker'. At about the fifth hour in the morning, take the end of the shadow cast by this gnomon, and mark it with a point. Then, opening your compasses to this point which marks the length of the gnomon's shadow, describe a circle from the centre. In the afternoon watch the shadow of your gnomon as it lengthens, and when it once more touches the circumference of this circle and the shadow in the afternoon is equal in length to that of the morning, mark it with a point.

7. From these two points describe with your compasses intersecting arcs, and through their intersection and the centre let a line be drawn to the circumference of the circle to give us the quarters of south and north. Then, using a sixteenth part of the entire circumference of the circle as a diameter, describe a circle with its centre on the line to the south, at the point where it crosses the circumference, and put points to the right and left on the circumference on the south side, repeating the process on the north side. From the four points thus obtained draw lines intersecting the centre from one side of the circumference

to the other. Thus we shall have an eighth part of the circumference set out for Auster and another for Septentrio. The rest of the entire circumference is then to be divided into three equal parts on each side, and thus we have designed a figure equally apportioned among the eight winds. Then let the directions of your streets and alleys be laid down on the lines of division between the quarters of two winds.

8. On this principle of arrangement the disagreeable force of the winds will be shut out from dwellings and lines of houses. For if the streets run full in the face of the winds, their constant blasts rushing in from the open country, and then confined by narrow alleys, will sweep through them with great violence. The lines of houses must therefore be directed away from the quarters from which the winds blow, so that as they come in they may strike against the angles of the blocks and their force thus be broken and dispersed.

216.

0. *Calm*
Sea like a mirror. Smoke rises vertically.
1. *Light Air*
Ripples with appearance of scales are formed, without foam crests. Direction shown by smoke drift but not by wind vanes.
2. *Light Breeze*
Small wavelets, still short, but not pronounced. Crests have a glassy appearance but do not break. Wind felt on face, leaves rustle, ordinary vanes moved by wind
3. *Gentle Breeze*
Large wavelets. Crests begin to break. Foam of glassy appearance. Perhaps scattered white horses. Leaves and small twigs in constant motion; wind extends light flag.
4. *Moderate*
Small waves, becoming larger; fairly frequent white horses. Breeze raises dust and loose paper, small branches are moved.
5. *Fresh Breeze*
Moderate waves, taking a more pronounced long form; many white horses are formed. Small trees in leaf begin to sway; crested wavelets form on inland waters.

6. *Strong Breeze*

Large waves begin to form; the white foam crests are more extensive everywhere. Large branches in motion; whistling heard in telegraph wires; umbrellas used with difficulty.

7. *Near Gale*

Sea heaps up and white foam from breaking waves begins to be blown in streaks along the direction of the wind. Whole trees in motion; inconvenience felt when walking against the wind.

8. *Gale*

Moderately high waves of greater length; edges of crests begin to break into spindrift. The foam is blown in well-marked streaks along the direction of the wind. Breaks twigs off trees; generally impedes progress.

9. *Severe Gale*

High waves. Dense streaks of foam along the direction of the wind. Crests of waves begin to topple, tumble and roll over. Spray may affect visibility. Slight structural damage (chimney-pots and slates removed).

10. *Storm*

Very high waves with long overhanging crests. The resulting foam, in great patches, is blown in dense white streaks along the direction of the wind. On the whole the surface of the sea takes on a white appearance. The tumbling of the sea becomes heavy and shock-like. Visibility affected. Seldom experienced inland; trees uprooted; considerable structural damage occurs.

11. *Violent Storm*

Exceptionally high waves (small and medium-sized ships might be for a time lost to view behind the waves). The sea is completely covered with long white patches of foam lying along the direction of the wind. Everywhere the edges of the wave crests are blown into froth. Visibility affected. Very rarely experienced; accompanied by widespread damage.

12. *Hurricane*

The air is filled with foam and spray. Sea completely white with driving spray; visibility very seriously affected.

217.

Sometimes I,
I go about pitying myself
While I am carried by the wind
Across the sky.

218.

26th Oct–7th Nov, 1703. The effects of the hurricane and tempest of
wind, rain, and lightning, through all the nation, especially London,
were very dismal. Many houses demolished, and people killed. As to
my own losses, the subversion of woods and timber, both ornamental
and valuable, through my whole estate, and about my house the
woods crowning the garden mount, and growing along the park
meadow, the damage to my own dwelling, farms, and outhouses, is
almost tragical, not to be paralleled with anything happening in our
age. I am not able to describe it; but submit to the pleasure of
Almighty God (…)

Methinks I still hear, and am sure feel, the dismal Groans
(happening on the 26th of *Novemb.* 1703) of our *Forests*, so many
thousand of goodly *Oakes* subverted by that late dreadful *Hurricane*;
prostrating the Trees, and crushing all that grew under them, lying in
ghastly Postures, like whole *Regiments* fallen in *Battel* by the Sword of
the *Conqueror*…

219.

It cannot but be needful to the present Design to Note that the
Difference in the Opinions of the Ancients, about the Nature and
Original of Winds, is a leading Step to one Assertion which I have
advanc'd, in all that I have said with Relation to Winds, *viz.* that there
seems to be more of God in the whole Appearance, than in any other
Part of Operating Nature.

Those Ancient Men of Genius who rifled Nature by the torch-
light of Reason even to her very Nudities, have been run a-ground in
this unknown Channel; the Wind has blown out the Candle of

Reason, and left them all in the Dark. The deepest Search into the Region of Cause and Consequence, has found out just enough to leave the wisest Philosopher in the dark, to bewilder his Head, and drown his Understanding. You raise a Storm in Nature by the very inquiry ...

Nor shall I often trouble the Reader with the Multitude or Magnitude of Trees blown down, whole Parks ruin'd, fine Walks defac'd, and Orchards laid flat, and the like: and tho' I had, myself, the Curiosity to count the Number of Trees, in a Circuit I rode, over most part of *Kent*, in which being tired with the Number, I left off reckoning after I had gone on to 17,000 ...

*

Above 400 Wind-mils overset, and broken to pieces; or the Sails so blown round, that the Timbers and Wheels have heated so as to set the rest on fire, and so burnt them down, as particularly several were in the Isle of *Ely*.

*

The sheets of Lead on *Lytton* Church, were rolled up like Sheets of Parchment, and blown off to a great Distance. At *Strode*, a large Apple Tree, being about a Foot in Square, was broken off cleverly like a Stick, about four Foot from the Root, and carried over an Hedge about ten Foot high; and cast, as if darted (with the Trunk forward), above fourteen Yards off.

*

The damage to the Thatch of Houses is so great and general, that the price of Reed arose from twenty shillings to fifty or three Pounds a Hundred; insomuch that to shelter themselves from the open Air, many poor People were glad to use Bean, Helm and Furze, to thatch their Houses with, Things never known to be put to such Use before.

As to stacks of Wheat, the Accounts are very strange — as of a great stack of Corn taken from the Hovel on which it stood, and without dislocating the Sheaves, set upon another Hovel, from whence the Wind had just before remov'd another Stack of equal Dimensions; [or] of a Stack of Wheat taken up with the Wind, and set down a whole 16 Rod off …

At *Cockeup*, two Miles from us… a great Oak of about nine or ten Loads was blown down, having a Raven sitting in it, his Wing-feathers got between two Boughs, and held him fast; but the Raven received no hurt.

In *Helford* [Devon], a small Haven, there was a Tin Ship blown from her Anchors with only one Man, and two Boys on Board, without Anchor, Cable or Boat, and was forc'd out of the said Haven about 12 o'clock at Night; the next Morning by 8 o'clock, the Ship miraculously Run in between two Rocks in the *Isle of Wight*, where the Men and Goods were saved, but the Ship lost.

220.

I could not even make out which was the sea, and which the sky, for the horizon seemed drunk, and was flying wildly about in all directions… when everything was sliding and bumping about, and when it did seem difficult to comprehend the possibility of anything afloat being more disturbed, without toppling over and going down. But what the agitation of a steam-vessel is, on a bad winter's night in the wild Atlantic, it is impossible for the most vivid imagination to conceive. To say that she is flung down on her side in the waves, with her masts dipping into them, and that, springing up again, she rolls over on the other side, until a heavy sea strikes her with the noise of a hundred great guns, and hurls her back; that she stops and staggers, and shivers, as though stunned, and then, with a violent throbbing at her heart, darts onward like a monster goaded into madness, to be beaten down, and battered, and crushed, and leapt on by the angry sea; that thunder, lightning, hail and rain, and wind are all in fierce contention for the mastery; that every plank has its groan, every nail its shriek, and every drop of water in the great ocean its howling voice – is nothing. To say that all is grand, and all appalling and horrible in the last degree, is nothing. Words cannot express it. Thoughts cannot convey it.

221.

A headlong savage southeastern squall
And night and the waves Orion whips up
When it sets in dark November
Were my downfall.
I, Callaiskhros, slipped out of life
Sailing the deep-sea shelf off Libya.
Now I am lost, swirled here and there,
A miserable prey to the fishes.

The stone on my grave claims
'Callaiskhros lies here.'
What a lie.

222.

Whirl up, sea —
whirl your pointed pines,
splash your great pines
on our rocks,
hurl your green over us,
cover us with your pools of fir.

223.

God thundereth marvellously with his voice; great things doeth he, which we cannot comprehend.

For he saith to the snow, Be thou on the earth; likewise to the small rain, and to the great rain of his strength.

He sealeth up the hand of every man; that all men may know his work.

Then the beasts go into dens: and remain in their places.

Out of the south cometh the whirlwind: and cold out of the north.

By the breath of God frost is given: and the breadth of the waters is straitened.

Also by watering he wearieth the thick cloud: he scattereth his bright cloud:

And it is turned round about by his counsels: that they may do whatsoever he commandeth them upon the face of the world in the earth.

He causeth it to come, whether for correction, or for his land, or for mercy.

Hearken unto this, O Job: stand still, and consider the wondrous works of God.

Dost thou know when God disposed them, and caused the light of his cloud to shine?

Dost thou know the balancings of the clouds, the wondrous works of him which is perfect in knowledge?

How thy garments are warm, when he quieteth the earth by the south wind?

Hast thou with him spread out the sky, which is strong, and as a molten looking glass?

Teach us what we shall say unto him; for we cannot order our speech by reason of darkness.

Shall it be told him that I speak? if a man speak, surely he shall be swallowed up.

And now men see not the bright light which is in the clouds: but the wind passeth, and cleanseth them.

Fair weather cometh out of the north: with God is terrible majesty.

224.

(*The heath. Before a hovel.*)

KING LEAR. First let me talke with this Philosopher. What is the cause of Thunder?

225.

The thunder mutters louder & more loud
With quicker motion hay folks ply the rake
Ready to burst slow sails the pitch black cloud
& all the gang a bigger haycock make
To sit beneath—the woodland winds awake
The drops so large wet all thro' in an hour
A tiney flood runs down the leaning rake
In the sweet hay yet dry the hay folks cower
& some beneath the waggon shun the shower

226.

When at last the sky fearfully rolled with thunder and flashed with lightning, as could not but follow from the bursting upon the air for the first time of an impression so violent, (…) thereupon a few giants, who must have been the most robust, and who were dispersed through the forests on the mountain heights where the strongest beasts have their dens, were frightened and astonished by the great effect whose cause they did not know, and raising their eyes became aware of the sky. And because in such a case the nature of the human mind leads it to attribute to its own nature the effect, and because in that early state their nature was to be men of robust bodily strength, who expressed their violent passions by shouting and grumbling, they pictured the sky to themselves as a great animated body, which in that aspect they called Jove, the first god of the so-called *gentes maiores*, who meant to tell them something by the hissing of his bolts and the clap of his thunder. And thus they began to exercise that natural curiosity which is the daughter of ignorance and the mother of knowledge, and which, opening the mind of man, gives birth to wonder.

227.

Where wast thou when I laid the foundations of the earth? declare, if thou hast understanding.

Who hath laid the measures thereof, if thou knowest? or who hath stretched the line upon it?

Whereupon are the foundations thereof fastened? or who laid the corner stone thereof;

When the morning stars sang together, and all the sons of God shouted for joy?

Or who shut up the sea with doors, when it brake forth, as if it had issued out of the womb?

When I made the cloud the garment thereof, and thick darkness a swaddling band for it,

And brake up for it my decreed place, and set bars and doors,

And said, Hitherto shalt thou come, but no further: and here shall thy proud waves be stayed? (…)

Hast thou entered into the treasures of the snow? or hast thou seen the treasures of the hail,

Which I have reserved against the time of trouble, against the day of battle and war?

By what way is the light parted, which scattereth the east wind upon the earth?

Who hath divided a watercourse for the overflowing of waters, or a way for the lightning of thunder;

To cause it to rain on the earth, where no man is; on the wilderness, wherein there is no man;

To satisfy the desolate and waste ground; and to cause the bud of the tender herb to spring forth?

Hath the rain a father? or who hath begotten the drops of dew?

Out of whose womb came the ice? and the hoary frost of heaven, who hath gendered it?

The waters are hid as with a stone, and the face of the deep is frozen.

Canst thou bind the sweet influences of Pleiades, or loose the bands of Orion?

Canst thou bring forth Mazzaroth in his season? or canst thou guide Arcturus with his sons?

Knowest thou the ordinances of heaven? canst thou set the dominion thereof in the earth?

Canst thou lift up thy voice to the clouds, that abundance of waters may cover thee?

Canst thou send lightnings, that they may go, and say unto thee, Here we are? (...)

Who can number the clouds in wisdom, or who can stay the bottles of heaven, when the dust grows into hardness, and the clods cleave fast together?

228.

I have been noting events forty years.

On the twentyseventh May eleven hundred
and seventyseven, eight p.m., fire broke out
at the corner of Tomi and Higuchi streets.
In a night
palace, ministries, university, parliament
were destroyed. As the wind veered
flames spread out in the shape of an open fan.
Tongues torn by gusts stretched and leapt.
In the sky clouds of cinders lit red with the blaze.
Some choked, some burned, some barely escaped.
Sixteen great officials lost houses and
very many poor. A third of the city burned;
several thousands died; and of beasts,
limitless numbers.

Men are fools to invest in real estate.

Three years less three days later a wind
starting near the outer boulevard
broke a path a quarter mile across
to Sixth Avenue.
Not a house stood. Some were felled whole,
some in splinters; some had left
great beams upright in the ground
and round about
lay rooves scattered where the wind flung them.
Flocks of furniture in the air,

everything flat fluttered like dead leaves.
A dust like fog or smoke,
you could hear nothing for the roar,
   bufera infernal!
Lamed some, wounded some.
This cyclone turned southwest.

Massacre without cause.

Portent?

The same year thunderbolted change of capital,
fixed here, Kyoto, for ages.
Nothing compelled the change nor was it an easy matter
but the grumbling was disproportionate.
We moved, those with jobs
or wanting jobs or hangers on of the rest,
in haste haste fretting to be the first.
Rooftrees overhanging empty rooms;
dismounted: floating down the river.
The soil returned to heath.

I visited the new site: narrow and too uneven,
cliffs and marshes, deafening shores, perpetual strong winds;
the palace a logcabin dumped amongst the hills
(yet not altogether inelegant).
There was no flat place for houses, many vacant lots,
the former capital wrecked, the new a camp,
and thoughts like clouds changing, frayed by a breath:
peasants bewailing lost land, newcomers aghast at prices.
No one in uniform: the crowds
resembled demobilized conscripts.

There were murmurs. Time defined them.
In the winter the decree was rescinded,
we returned to Kyoto;
but the houses were gone and none
could afford to rebuild them.

I have heard of a time when kings beneath bark rooves
watched chimneys.
When smoke was scarce, taxes were remitted.

To appreciate present conditions,
collate them with those of antiquity.

229.

(*The Angel leads Adam up to a high Hill, sets before him in vision what shall happen till the Flood*)

>   … but of God observ'd
The one just Man alive, by his command
Shall build a wondrous Ark, as thou beheldst,
To save himself and houshold from amidst
A World devote to universal rack.
No sooner hee with them of Man and Beast
Select for life shall in the Ark be lodg'd,
And shelterd round, but all the Cataracts
Of Heav'n set open on the Earth shall powre
Raine day and night, all fountains of the Deep
Broke up, shall heave the Ocean to usurp
Beyond all bounds, till inundation rise
Above the highest Hills: then shall this Mount
Of Paradise by might of Waves be moov'd
Out of his place, push'd by the hornèd floud,
With all his verdure spoil'd, and Trees adrift
Down the great River to the op'ning Gulf,
And there take root an Iland salt and bare,
The haunt of Seales and Orcs, and Sea-mews clang.

230.

When *Jove* behelde how all the world stood lyke a plash of raine,
And of so many thousand men and women did remaine
But one of eche, howbeit those both just and both devout,

He brake the cloudes, and did commaund that *Boreas* with his stout
And sturdie blasts should chase the floud, that Earth might see the skie
And Heaven the Earth: the Seas also began immediatly
Their raging furie for to cease. Their ruler laide awaye
His dreadfull Mace, and with his wordes their woodnesse did allaye.
He callèd *Triton* to him straight, his trumpetter, who stoode
In purple robe on shoulder cast, aloft upon the floode,
And bade him take his sounding Trumpe and out of hand to blow
Retreat, that all the streames might heare, and cease from thence to flow.
He tooke his Trumpet in his hand, hys Trumpet was a shell
Of some great Whelke or other fishe, in fashion like a Bell
That gathered narrow to the mouth, and as it did descende
Did waxe more wide and writhen still, downe to the nether ende:
When that this Trump amid the sea was set to *Tritons* mouth,
He blew so loude that all the streames both East, West, North and South
Might easly heare him blow retreate, and all that heard the sound
Immediatly began to ebbe and draw within their bound.
Then gan the Sea to have a shore, and brookes to fynde a banke,
And swelling streames of flowing flouds within hir channels sanke.
Then hils did rise above the waves that had them overflow,
And as the waters did decrease, the ground did seeme to grow.
And after long and tedious time the trees did shew their tops
All bare, save that upon the boughes the mud did hang in knops.
The world restorèd was again...

231.

(*The Rain Man praises himself*)

No house is ever too thick-built
To keep me, the rain, from getting in.
I am well-known to huts and roofs,
A grandson of Never-Been-There.
I am mother of the finest grasses,
Father of green fields everywhere.
My arrows do not miss their aim,
They strike the owners of huts.
I am a terror to clay walls and the architecture of termites,

Fear-inspiring above and below.
When I pour in the morning, people say:
'He has cut off our lips and stopped our mouths,
He is giving us juicy fruits.
He has rained and brought us mushrooms,
White as ivory.'

232.

The King's most Excellent Majesty taking into His Pious and Princely
consideration, that great and immoderate Rains and Waters have
lately fallen in the Land, whereupon it may be feared, scarcity, and
famine, and sickness and diseases will ensue, if Almighty God of his
great Clemency be not mercifully pleased to avert those Judgements
and Punishments, which our many and manifold sins and
provocations have justly deserved:

And his Majesty having assembled His high Court of Parliament (the
Representative Body of this Kingdom) which is now sitting, and being
thereto moved by the Petition of both the Houses of Lords and
Commons in Parliament, and out of His own Religious disposition
readily inclined, hath resolved, and hereby doth Command a general
and publick Fast to be kept throughout this whole Kingdom, in such
manner as hereafter is directed and prescribed, that so both Prince and
People, even the whole Kingdom, as one man, may send up their Prayers
and Supplications to Almighty God, to divert those Judgements which
the sins of this Land have worthily deserved, and to continue the blessed
change of weather now begun, and to offer up to him their hearty and
unfained thanks for this, and other abundant mercies formerly
vouchsafed unto them, and to beseech his blessing upon that great
Assembly of this Nation, and to prosper their actions and endeavours.

233.

26th March, 1699. After an extraordinary storm, there came up the
Thames a whale which was fifty-six feet long. Such, and a larger of the
spout kind, was killed there forty years ago (June 1658). That year
died Cromwell.

234.

How finely dost thou times and seasons spin.
And make a twist checker'd with night and day!
Which as it lengthens windes, and windes us in,
As bowls go on, but turning all the way.

235.

God made Sun and Moon to distinguish seasons, and day, and night,
and we cannot have the fruits of the earth but in their seasons: But
God hath made no decree to distinguish the seasons of his mercies;
In paradise, the fruits were ripe, the first minute, and in heaven it is
alwaies Autumne, his mercies are ever in their maturity. We ask
panem quotidianum, our daily bread, and God never sayes you
should have come yesterday, he never sayes you must againe
to-morrow, but *today if you will heare his voice*, today he will heare
you.
　　If some King of the earth have so large an extent of Dominion,
in North, and South, as that he hath Winter and Summer together
in his Dominions, so large an extent East and West, as that he hath
day and night together in his Dominions, much more hath God
mercy and judgement together: He brought light out of darknesse,
not out of a lesser light; he can bring thy Summer out of Winter,
though thou have no Spring; though in the wayes of fortune, or
understanding, or conscience, thou have been benighted till now,
wintred and frozen, clouded and eclypsed, damped and
benummed, smothered and stupified till now, now God comes to
thee, not as in the dawning of the day, not as in the bud of the
spring, but as the Sun at noon to illustrate all shadowes, as the
sheaves in harvest, to fill all penuries, all occasions invite his
mercies, and all times are his seasons.

236.

I would gladly sacrifice part of my life to know the average barometer
reading in Paradise.

237.

Thus are the world's enclosures open lay'd,
And the vast space, where all things moove, display'd,
The habitations of celestial powers,
Neither shaken with winds, nor wett with showers,
Which snows do not infest, white frosts, nor haile,
Where no darke clouds heavn's constant splendor vaile,
Where light dilateth smiles on every side,
Where all by their owne nature are supplied,
Where no disturbance ever can molest
The sacred peace, with which the mind is blest.
And then againe hell's kingdomes nowhere do
Appeare (for earth doth not resist our view
Of that vast deepe, which underneath it lies).
What sweete delight and wonder did surprize
My thoughts, when thus I found nature disclos'd,
And by THY skill to mortalls' sight expos'd!

238.

Whan that Aprille with his shoures soote,
The droghte of March hath perced to the roote,
And bathed every veyne in swich licóur
Of which vertú engendred is the flour;
Whan Zephirus eek with his swete breeth
Inspired hath in every holt and heeth
The tendre croppes, and the yonge sonne
Hath in the Ram his halfe cours y-ronne,
And smale foweles maken melodye,
That slepen al the nyght with open ye,
So priketh hem Natúre in hir corages,
Thanne longen folk to goon on pilgrimages,
And palmeres for to seken straunge strondes,
To ferne halwes, kowthe in sondry londes;
And specially, from every shires ende
Of Engelond, to Caunterbury they wende,
The hooly blisful martir for to seke,
That hem hath holpen whan that they were seeke.

239.

(Gawain journeys North)

Now rides this renk thurgh the ryalme of Logres,
Sir Gauan, on Godes halve, thagh hym no gomen thoght.
Oft leudles alone he lenges on nyghtes
Ther he fonde noght hym byfore the fare that he lyked.
Hade he no fere bot his fole bi frythes and dounes,
Ne no gome bot God bi gate wyth to karp,
Til that he neghed ful neghe into the Northe Wales.
Alle the iles of Anglesay on lyft half he haldes,
And fares over the fordes by the forlondes,
Over at the Holy-Hede, til he hade eft bonk
In the wyldrenesse of Wyrale; woned ther bot lyte
That auther God other gome wyth goud hert lovied.

(…)

Mony klyf he overclambe in contrayes straunge,
Fer floten fro his frendes fremedly he rydes.
At uche warthe other water ther the wye passed
He fonde a foo hym byfore, bot ferly hit were,
And that so foule and so felle that fyght hym behoved.
So mony mervayl bi mount ther the mon fyndes,
Hit were to tore for to telle of the tenthe dole.
Sumwhyle wyth wormes he werres, and with wolves als,
Sumwhyle wyth wodwos, that woned in the knarres,
Bothe wyth bulles and beres, and bores otherwhyle,
And etaynes, that hym anelede of the heghe felle;
Nade he ben doghty and drye, and Dryghtyn had served,
Douteles he hade ben ded and dreped ful ofte.
For werre wrathed hym not so much that wynter nas wors,
When the colde cler water fro the cloudes schadde,
And fres er hit falle myght to the fale erthe;
Ner slayn wyth the slete he sleped in his yrnes
Mo nyghtes than innoghe in naked rokkes,
Ther as claterande fro the crest the colde borne rennes,
And henged heghe over his hede in hard iisse-ikkles.

240.

Arrived at the Grindenwald — dined — mounted again & rode to the
higher Glacier — twilight — but distinct — very fine Glacier — like a
frozen hurricane — Starlight — beautiful — but a devil of a path —
never mind — got safe in — a little lightning — but the whole of the
day as fine in point of weather — as the day on which Paradise was
made. — Passed *whole woods of withered pines* — *all withered*
— trunks stripped & barkless — branches lifeless — done by a single
winter — their appearance reminded me of me & my family.

241.

Shine out, fair Sun, with all your heat,
Show all your thousand-coloured light!
Black Winter freezes to his seat;
The grey wolf howls, he does so bite;
Crookt Age on three knees creeps the street;
The boneless fish close quaking lies
And eats for cold his aching feet;
The stars in icicles arise:
Shine out, and make this winter night
Our beauty's Spring, our Prince of Light!

242.

In the far north, where the taiga meets the treeless tundra, among the
dwarf birches, the low-growing rowan bushes with their surprisingly
large bright yellow, juicy berries, and the six-hundred-year-old
larches (they reach maturity at three hundred years), there is a special
tree, the dwarf pine. It is a distant relative of the Siberian cedar or
pine, an evergreen bush with a trunk that is thicker than a human
arm and two or three metres long. It does not mind where it grows;
its roots will cling to cracks in the rocks on mountain slopes. It is
manly and stubborn, like all northern trees. And sensitive.

It is late autumn and snow and winter are long overdue. For many
days there have been low, bluish clouds moving along the edge of the

white horizon: storm clouds that look as if they are covered in bruises. This morning the piercing autumn wind has turned ominously quiet. Is there a hint of snow? No. There won't be any snow. The dwarf pine has not bent down yet. Days pass, and still there is no snow and the heavy clouds wander about somewhere behind the bare hills, while a small pale sun has risen, in the high sky, and everything is as it should be in autumn.

Then the dwarf pine bends. It bends lower and lower, as if under an immense ever-increasing weight. Its crown scratches the rock and huddles against the ground as it stretches out its emerald paws. It is making its bed. It is like an octopus dressed in green feathers. Once it has lain down, it waits a day or two, and now the white sky delivers a shower of snow like powder, and the dwarf pine sinks into hibernation, like a bear. Enormous snowy blisters swell up on the white mountain: the dwarf pine bushes in their winter sleep.

243.

One must have a mind of winter
To regard the frost and the boughs
Of the pine-trees crusted with snow;

And have been cold a long time
To behold the junipers shagged with ice,
The spruces rough in the distant glitter

Of the January sun; and not to think
Of any misery in the sound of the wind,
In the sound of a few leaves,

Which is the sound of the land
Full of the same wind
That is blowing in the same bare place

For the listener, who listens in the snow,
And, nothing himself, beholds
Nothing that is not there and the nothing that is.

244.

My comforts drop and melt away like snow:
I shake my head, and all the thoughts and ends,
Which my fierce youth did bandie, fall and flow
Like leaves about me: or like summer friends,
Flyes of estates and sunne-shine. But to all
Who think me eager, hot, and undertaking,
But in my prosecutions slack and small;
As a young exhalation, newly waking,
Scorns his first bed of dirt, and means the sky;
But cooling by the way, grows pursie and slow,
And setling to a cloud, doth live and die
In that dark state of tears: to all, that so
   Show me, and set me, I have one reply,
   Which they that know the rest, know more than I.

245.

And this was, as thise bookes me remembre,
The colde, frosty seson of Decembre.
Phebus wax old, and hewed lyk laton,
That in his hoote declynacion
Shoon as the burned gold with stremes brighte;
But now in Capricorn adoun he lighte,
Where as he shoon ful pale, I dar wel seyn.
The bittre frostes, with the sleet and reyn,
Destroyed hath the grene in every yerd.
Janus sit by the fyr, with double berd,
And drynketh of his bugle horn the wyn;
Biforn hym stant brawen of the tusked swyn,
And 'Nowel' crieth every lusty man.

246.

So great, for instance, is the contrast between our climate and the
climates which we have described that the difference, when
considered in detail, surpasses belief. For example, there are

countries where, because of the excessive cold, the greatest rivers are frozen over, the ice sustaining the crossing of armies and the passage of heavily laden wagons, the wine and all other juices freeze so that they must be cut with knives, yea, what is more wonderful still, the extremities of human beings fall off when rubbed by the clothing, their eyes are blinded, fire furnishes no protection, even bronze statues are cracked open, and at certain seasons, they say, the clouds are so thick that in those regions there is neither lightning nor thunder; and many other things, more astonishing than these, come to pass, which are unbelievable to such as are ignorant of them, and cannot be endured by any who have actually experienced them...

Nevertheless, the inhabitants of the lands which we have mentioned, far from desiring to escape from the excessive evils which befall them, actually, on the contrary, give up their lives of their own accord simply to avoid being compelled to make trial of a different fare and manner of life. Thus it is that every country to which a man has grown accustomed holds a kind of spell of its own over him, and the length of time which he has spent there from infancy overcomes the hardship which he suffers from its climate.

247.

I have sent in accordance with your wishes the books about the man of God, Cuthbert, composed in verse and prose. And if I could have done more, I would gladly have done so. For the conditions of the past winter oppressed the island of our race very horribly with cold and ice, and long and widespread storms of wind and rain, so that the hand of the scribe was hindered from producing a great number of books.

248.

January 1886. Cold weather brings out upon the faces of people the written marks of their habits, vices, passions, and memories, as warmth brings out on paper a writing in sympathetic ink.

249.

In to thir dirk and drublie dayis,
Quhone sabill all the Hevin arrayis
With mystie vapouris, cluddis and skyis,
Nature all curage me denyis
Off sangis, ballattis, and of playis.

Quhone that the nycht dois lenth in houris,
With wind, with haill, and havy schouris,
My dule spreit dois lurk for schoir.
My hairt for langour dois forloir,
For laik of Symmer with his flouris.

I walk, I turne, sleip may I nocht,
I vexit am with havie thocht.
This warld all ouir I cast about,
And ay the mair I am in dout,
The mair that I remeid have socht.

I am assayit on everie syde.
Despair sayis ay, 'In tyme provyde
And get sum thing quhairon to leif,
Or with grit trouble and mischeif
Thow sall into this court abyd.'

Than Patience sayis, 'Be not agast,
Hald Hoip and Treuthe within thee fast,
And lat Fortoun wirk furthe hir rage,
Quhone that no rasoun may assuage
Quhill that hir glas be run and past.'

And Prudence in my eir sayis ay,
'Quhy wald thow hald that will away,
Or craif that thow may have no space,
Thow tending to ane uther place,
A journay going everie day?'

And than sayis Age, 'My freind, cum neir,
And be not strange, I thee requeir.
Cum, brodir, by the hand me tak.
Remember thow hes compt to mak
Of all thi tyme thow spendit heir.'

Syne Deid castis upe his yettis wyd
Saying, 'Thir oppin sall thee abyd;
Albeid that thow wer never sa stout,
Undir this lyntall sall thow lowt –
Thair is nane uther way besyde.'

For feir of this all day I drowp.
No gold in kist nor wine in cowp,
No ladeis bewtie nor luiffis blys
May lat me to remember this,
How glaid that ever I dyne or sowp.

Yit quone the nycht begynnis to schort
It dois my spreit sum pairt confort,
Off thocht oppressit with the schowris.
Cum, lustie Symmer, with thi flowris,
That I may leif in sum disport.

250.

In April, and the Springtime, his Lordship would, when it rayned,
take his Coach (open) to receive the benefit of Irrigation, which he
was wont to say was very wholsome because of the Nitre in the Aire
and the Universall Spirit of the World.

Mr. Hobbs told me that the cause of his Lordship's death was
trying an Experiment; viz. as he was taking the aire in a Coach with
Dr. Witherborne (a Scotchman, Physician to the King) towards
Highgate, snow lay on the ground, and it came into my Lord's
thoughts, why Flesh might not be preserved in snow, as in Salt. They
were resolved they would try the Experiment presently. They alighted
out of the Coach and went into a poore woman's house at the bottom

of Highgate hill, and bought a Hen, and made the woman exenterate it, and then stuffed the body with Snow, and my Lord did help to doe it himselfe. The Snow so chilled him that he immediately fell so extremely ill, that he could not returne to his Lodging (I suppose then at Graye's Inne) but went to the Earl of Arundel's house at Highgate, where they put him into a good bed warmed with a Panne, but it was a damp bed that had not been layn-in in about a year before, which gave him such a cold that in 2 or 3 dayes as I remember he told me, he dyed of Suffocation.

251.

Near the Vipsanian columns where the aqueduct
    drips down the side of its dark arch,
the stone is a green and pulsing velvet
    and the air is powdered with sweat
from the invisible faucet: there winter
    shaped a dagger of ice, waited till
a boy looked up at the quondam stalactites,
    threw it like a gimlet through his throat
and as in a murder in a paperback the clever
    weapon melted away in its own hole. Where
have blood and water flowed before from one wound?
    The story is trivial and the instance holy –
what portion of power has violent fortune
    ever surrendered, what degraded circumstance
will she refuse? Death is everywhere
    if water, the life-giving element,
will descend to cutting throats.

252.

There were some circumstances attending the remarkable frost in January 1776 so singular and striking, that a short detail of them may not be unacceptable. The most certain way to be exact will be to copy the passages from my journal, which were taken from time to time as things occurred.

January 7th. – Snow driving all the day, which was followed by frost, sleet, and some snow, till the 12th, when a prodigious mass overwhelmed all the works of men, drifting over the tops of the gates and filling the hollow lanes.

On the 14th the writer was obliged to be much abroad; and thinks he never before or since has encountered such rugged Siberian weather. Many of the narrow roads were now filled above the tops of the hedges; through which the snow was driven into most romantic and grotesque shapes, so striking to the imagination as not to be seen without wonder and pleasure. The poultry dared not to stir out of their roosting-places; for cocks and hens are so dazzled and confounded by the glare of snow that they would soon perish without assistance. The hares also lay sullenly in their seats, and would not move until compelled by hunger; being conscious, poor animals, that the drifts and heaps treacherously betray their footsteps, and prove fatal to numbers of them.

From the 14th the snow continued to increase, and began to stop the road waggons and coaches, which could no longer keep on their regular stages; and especially on the western roads, where the fall appears to have been deeper than in the south. The company at Bath, that wanted to attend the Queen's birth-day, were strangely incommoded: many carriages of persons, who got, in their way to town from Bath, as far as Marlborough, after strange embarrassments, here met with a ne plus ultra. The ladies fretted, and offered large rewards to labourers, if they would shovel them a track to London; but the relentless heaps of snow were too bulky to be removed; and so the 18th passed over, leaving the company in very uncomfortable circumstances at the Castle and other inns.

On the 20th the sun shone out for the first time since the frost began; a circumstance that has been remarked before much in favour of vegetation. All this time the cold was not very intense, for the thermometer stood at 29, 28, 25, and thereabout; but on the 21st it descended to 20. The birds now began to be in a very pitiable and starving condition. Tamed by the season, skylarks settled in the streets of towns, because they saw the ground was bare; rooks frequented dunghills close to houses; and crows watched horses as they passed, and greedily devoured what dropped from them; hares now came into men's gardens, and, scraping away the snow, devoured such plants as they could find.

On the 22nd the author had occasion to go to *London* through a sort of *Laplandian-scene*, very wild and grotesque indeed. But the metropolis itself exhibited a still more singular appearance than the country; for, being bedded deep in snow, the pavement of the streets could not be touched by the wheels or the horses' feet, so that the carriages ran about without the least noise. Such an exception from din and clatter was strange, but not pleasant; it seemed to convey an uncomfortable idea of desolation:

> ... *ipsa silentia terrent.*

(...) During these four nights the cold was so penetrating that it occasioned ice in warm chambers and under beds; and in the day the wind was so keen that persons of robust constitutions could scarcely endure to face it. The Thames was at once so frozen over both above and below bridge that crowds ran about on the ice. The streets were now strangely incumbered with snow, which crumbled and trod dusty; and, turning grey, resembled bay-salt; what had fallen on the roofs was so perfectly dry that, from first to last, it lay twenty-six days on the houses in the city; a longer time than had been remembered by the oldest housekeepers living. According to all appearances we might now have expected the continuance of this rigorous weather for weeks to come, since every night increased in severity; but behold, without any apparent cause, on the 1st of February a thaw took place, and some rain followed before night; making good the observation above, that frosts often go off as it were at once, without any gradual declension of cold. On the second of February the thaw persisted; and on the 3d swarms of little insects were frisking and sporting in a court-yard at South Lambeth, as if they had felt no frost. Why the juices in the small bodies and smaller limbs of such minute beings are not frozen is a matter of curious inquiry.

253.

The Great Frost was, historians tell us, the most severe that has
ever visited these islands. Birds froze in mid-air and fell like
stones to the ground. At Norwich a young countrywoman started
to cross the road in her usual robust health and was seen by the
onlookers to turn visibly to powder and be blown in a puff of dust
over the roofs as the icy blast struck her at the street corner. The
mortality among sheep and cattle was enormous. Corpses froze
and could not be drawn from the sheets. It was no uncommon
sight to come upon a whole herd of swine frozen immovable upon
the road. The fields were full of shepherds, ploughmen, teams of
horses, and little bird-scaring boys all struck stark in the act of the
moment, one with his hand to his nose, another with the bottle to
his lips, a third with a stone raised to throw at the raven who sat,
as if stuffed, upon the hedge within a yard of him. The severity of
the frost was so extraordinary that a kind of petrifaction
sometimes ensued; and it was commonly supposed that the great
increase of rocks in some parts of Derbyshire was due to no
eruption, for there was none, but to the solidification of
unfortunate wayfarers who had been turned literally to stone
where they stood. The Church could give little help in the matter,
and though some landowners had these relics blessed, the most
part preferred to use them either as landmarks, scratching-posts
for sheep, or, when the form of the stone allowed, drinking
troughs for cattle, which purposes they serve, admirably for the
most part, to this day.

(...) The new King seized the opportunity that his coronation
gave him to curry favour with the citizens. He directed that the
river, which was frozen to a depth of twenty feet and more for six
or seven miles on either side, should be swept, decorated and
given all the semblance of a park or pleasure ground, with arbours,
mazes, alleys, drinking booths, etc. at his expense. For himself and
the courtiers, he reserved a certain space immediately opposite the
Palace gates; which, railed off from the public only by a silken
rope, became at once the centre of the most brilliant society in
England.

254.

There are strange things done in the midnight sun
By the men who moil for gold;
The Arctic trails have their secret tales
That would make your blood run cold;
The Northern Lights have seen queer sights,
But the queerest they ever did see
Was that night on the marge of Lake Lebarge
I cremated Sam McGee.

Now Sam McGee was from Tennessee, where the cotton blooms and blows.
Why he left his home in the South to roam 'round the Pole, God only knows.
He was always cold, but the land of gold seemed to hold him like a spell;
Though he'd often say in his homely way that he'd 'sooner live in hell'.

On a Christmas Day we were mushing our way over the Dawson trail.
Talk of your cold! through the parka's fold it stabbed like a driven nail.
If our eyes we'd close, then the lashes froze till sometimes we couldn't see;
It wasn't much fun, but the only one to whimper was Sam McGee.

And that very night, as we lay packed tight in our robes beneath the snow,
And the dogs were fed, and the stars o'erhead were dancing heel and toe,
He turned to me, and 'Cap,' says he, 'I'll cash in this trip, I guess;
And if I do, I'm asking that you won't refuse my last request.'

Well, he seemed so low that I couldn't say no; then he says with a sort of moan:
'It's the cursèd cold, and it's got right hold till I'm chilled clean through to the bone.
Yet 'tain't being dead – it's my awful dread of the icy grave that pains;
So I want you to swear that, foul or fair, you'll cremate my last remains.'

A pal's last need is a thing to heed, so I swore I would not fail;
And we started on at the streak of dawn; but God! he looked ghastly pale.
He crouched on the sleigh, and he raved all day of his home in Tennessee;
And before nightfall a corpse was all that was left of Sam McGee.

There wasn't a breath in that land of death, and I hurried, horror-driven,
With a corpse half hid that I couldn't get rid, because of a promise given;
It was lashed to the sleigh, and it seemed to say: 'You may tax your brawn and brains,
But you promised true, and it's up to you to cremate those last remains.'

Now a promise made is a debt unpaid, and the trail has its own stern code.
In the days to come, though my lips were dumb, in my heart how I cursed that load.
In the long, long night, by the lone firelight, while the huskies, round in a ring,
Howled out their woes to the homeless snows – O God! how I loathed the thing.

And every day that quiet clay seemed to heavy and heavier grow;
And on I went, though the dogs were spent and the grub was getting low;
The trail was bad, and I felt half mad, but I swore I would not give in;
And I'd often sing to the hateful thing, and it hearkened with a grin.

Till I came to the marge of Lake Lebarge, and a derelict there lay;
It was jammed in the ice, but I saw in a trice it was called the 'Alice May'.
And I looked at it, and I thought a bit, and I looked at my frozen chum;
Then 'Here,' said I, with a sudden cry, 'is my cre-ma-tor-eum.'

Some planks I tore from the cabin floor, and I lit the boiler fire;
Some coal I found that was lying around, and I heaped the fuel higher;
The flames just soared, and the furnace roared – such a blaze you seldom see;
And I burrowed a hole in the glowing coal, and I stuffed in Sam McGee.

Then I made a hike, for I didn't like to hear him sizzle so;
And the heavens scowled, and the huskies howled, and the wind began to blow.
It was icy cold, but the hot sweat rolled down my cheeks, and I don't know why;
And the greasy smoke in an inky cloak went streaking down the sky.

I do not know how long in the snow I wrestled with grisly fear;
But the stars came out and they danced about ere again I ventured near;
I was sick with dread, but I bravely said: 'I'll just take a peep inside.
I guess he's cooked, and it's time I looked' … then the door I opened wide.

And there sat Sam, looking cool and calm, in the heart of the furnace roar;
And he wore a smile you could see a mile, and he said: 'Please close that door.
It's fine in here, but I greatly fear you'll let in the cold and storm –
Since I left Plumtree, down in Tennessee, it's the first time I've been warm.'

> *There are strange things done in the midnight sun*
> *By the men who moil for gold;*
> *The Arctic trails have their secret tales*
> *That would make your blood run cold;*
> *The Northern Lights have seen queer sights,*
> *But the queerest they ever did see*
> *Was that night on the marge of Lake Lebarge*
> *I cremated Sam McGee.*

255.

At the extremity of our hemisphere one hears the sound of the sun
sinking beneath the waves... Beyond the country of the Swedes there
is another sea, sluggish and well-nigh motionless, which is believed to
be the boundary and limit of the world, because here the last glow of
the setting sun shines on into the following dawn, so as to dim the
brightness of the stars. Nay, further, we are told that the noise of the
sun rising out of the waters is heard, and that his attendant deities are
seen and his crown of rays.

256.

The waterbug is drawing the shadows of the evening
      toward him on the water.

257.

What are we to do with these spring days that are fast coming on?
Early this morning the sky was grey, but now if you go to the window
you are surprised, and lean your cheek against the window-latch.
      The sun is already setting, but down below you see it lighting up
the face of the young girl who just strolls along looking about her,
and at the same time you see her caught in the shadow of the man
behind overtaking her.
      And then the man has passed by and the face of the child is quite
bright.

258.

(Washington DC – 37th Congress, 3 March 1863). All the elements,
capricious, light and shadow, tears and smiles, today. Most of the
forenoon was beautiful exceedingly, bright sun, steady soft
atmosphere. At about noon, it grew very dark and cloudy, about 1 it
rained – from 2 to 3 we had a driving snow storm. I never saw flakes
larger – they drove and rampaged away – very good view from my
high window looking across to the Potomac, Arlington Heights, and

down to Alexandria. I watched this noble and peculiar storm for an hour – full of fine effects. (When it snows heavily, get into a high place, and look up into the air.) Soon after 3 it began to break. I saw the sun shining over in Old Virginia, away down toward Fairfax seminary, and all along shore, for some time while the storm was dark and driving all around where I stood at my high window watching it. Half past 3, it is all clear and bright again – yet almost as I jot this down the clouds come swiftly up. This is the last day of the 37th Congress, the body during whose existence (1861–63) the most important, confusing, and abnormal ? events in American history (shall I not say in the history of the world?) have happened.

The 37th Congress – As I have watched their debates, wrangles, propositions, personal presences, physiognomies, in their magnificent sky-lighted halls – gone night and day, sat, seen, listened – sometimes literally doubting for a moment my own eyes and ears – I have learned many new things. These then are the men who do as they do, in the midst of the greatest historic chaos and gigantic tussle of the greatest of ages. – Look at the little mannikins, shrewd, gabby, drest in black, hopping about, making motions, amendments. – It is very curious – At night I have gone in the gallery to look at them, down there, flooded with light stronger than sunshine, in the most magnificent, and best proportioned rooms in the world – What events are about them, and all of us? Whither are we drifting? Who knows? It seems as if these electric and terrible days were enough to put life in a paving stone – as if there must needs form, on the representative men that have to do with them, faces of grandeur, actions of awe, vestments of majesty – the day goes on, a strange, wild, smiling, promising, lowering, spitting day – full of threats and contradictions – black at times as murkyest eve – then snowing in great flakes, obscuring the air, with fits of furious driving, and of whirls and eddies around and around as you look up – then a sharp short shower of rain. It goes on and on – not without gleams, returns of repentance, a fine sky, with sunshine and much promise – but much disquiet too. Then at last, with a long wide breadth of heavy sombre slate and opaque iron or lead in the west, but with a thin belt below it, as of clearish water, crimsoned. And there the sun goes down in blood. It seems to be looking at These States, fratricidal states. It lingers, not glaring, but astonished, pained, shall I not say terrified – seems indeed to pause to pierce the wonder, the mystery and urged chaos of these lands, these days – but yet goes down in a flood.

259.

These sunsets differ in the nature of the glow, which is both intense and lustreless, and that both in the sky and in the earth. The glow is intense, this is what strikes everyone; it has prolonged the daylight, and optically changed the season; it bathes the whole sky, it is mistaken for the reflection of a great fire; at the sundown itself and southwards from that on December 4, I took a note of it as more like inflamed flesh than the lucid reds of ordinary sunsets. On the same evening the fields facing west glowed as if overlaid with yellow wax.

But it is also lustreless. A bright sunset lines the clouds so that their brims look like gold, brass, bronze, or steel. It fetches out those dazzling flecks and spangles which people call fish-scales. It gives to a mackerel or dappled cloudrack the appearance of quilted crimson silk, or a ploughed field glazed with crimson ice. These effects may have been seen in the late sunsets, but they are not the specific after-glow; that is, without gloss or lustre (...)

They differ in the regularity of their colouring. Four colours in particular have been noticeable in these after-glows, and in a fixed order of time and place – orange, lowest and nearest the sundown; above this, and broader, green; above this, broader still, a variable red, ending in being crimson; above this a faint lilac. The lilac disappears; the green deepens, spreads and encroaches on the orange; and the red deepens, spreads and encroaches on the green, till at last one red, varying downwards from crimson to scarlet or orange, fills the west and south (...)

Ordinary sunsets have not this order; this, so to say, fixed and limited palette. The green in particular, is low down when it appears. There is often a trace of olive between the sundown and the higher blue sky, but it never develops, that I remember, into a fresh green (...) The green is between apple-green or pea-green (which are pure greens) and an olive (which is tertiary colour): it is vivid and beautiful, but not pure. The red is very impure, and not evenly laid on. On the 4th it appeared brown, like a strong light behind tortoiseshell, or Derbyshire alabaster. It has been well compared to the colour of incandescent iron. Sometimes it appears like a mixture of chalk with sand and muddy earths. The pigments for it would be ochre and Indian red.

260.

It has been stated that certain flowers, towards evening in summer, coruscate, become phosphorescent, or emit a momentary light. Some persons have described their observation of this minutely. I had often endeavoured to witness it myself, and had even resorted to artificial contrivances to produce it.

On the 19th of June, 1799, late in the evening, when the twilight was deepening into a clear night, as I was walking up and down the garden with a friend, we very distinctly observed a flame-like appearance near the oriental poppy, the flowers of which are remarkable for their powerful red colour. We approached the place and looked attentively at the flowers, but could perceive nothing further, till at last, by passing and repassing repeatedly, while we looked sideways on them, we succeeded in renewing the appearance as often as we pleased. It proved to be a physiological phenomenon, such as others we have described, and the apparent coruscation was nothing but the spectrum of the flower in the compensatory blue-green colour.

261.

Either by day or a little after sunset in fine weather, a little, light, long-drawn cloud is seen, like a long very straight line.

262.

I was walking along the road with two friends – the sun was setting – I felt a wave of sadness – the sky suddenly turned blood-red. I stopped, leaned against the railing, tired to death – I looked out over the flaming clouds like blood and swords – the blue-black fjord and city – my friends walked on – I stood there trembling with angst – and I felt as though a vast, endless Scream passed through nature.

263.

The reach was narrow, straight, with high sides like a railway cutting. The dusk came gliding into it long before the sun had set. The current ran smooth and swift, but a dumb immobility sat on the banks. The living trees, lashed together by the creepers and every living bush of the undergrowth, might have been changed into stone, even to the slenderest twig, to the lightest leaf. It was not sleep – it seemed unnatural, like a state of trance. Not the faintest sound of any kind could be heard. You looked on amazed, and began to suspect yourself of being deaf – then the night came suddenly, and struck you blind as well. About three in the morning some large fish leapt, and the loud splash made me jump as though a gun had been fired. When the sun rose there was a white fog, very warm and clammy, and more blinding than the night. It did not shift or drive; it was just there, standing all round you like something solid. At eight or nine, perhaps, it lifted as a shutter lifts. We had a glimpse of the towering multitude of trees, of the immense matted jungle, with the blazing little ball of the sun hanging over it—all perfectly still—and then the white shutter came down again, smoothly, as if sliding in greased grooves. I ordered the chain, which we had begun to heave in, to be paid out again. Before it stopped running with a muffled rattle, a cry, a very loud cry, as of infinite desolation, soared slowly in the opaque air. It ceased. A complaining clamour, modulated in savage discords, filled our ears. The sheer unexpectedness of it made my hair stir under my cap. I don't know how it struck the others: to me it seemed as though the mist itself had screamed...

264.

Travelling in a comfortable car
Down a rainy road in the country
We saw a ragged fellow at nightfall
Signal to us for a ride, with a low bow.
We had a roof and we had room and we drove on
And we heard me say, in a grumpy voice: no
We can't take anyone with us.
We had gone on a long way, perhaps a day's march

When suddenly I was shocked by this voice of mine
This behaviour of mine and this
Whole world.

265.

Let us go then, you and I,
When the evening is spread out against the sky
Like a patient etherised upon a table;
Let us go, through certain half-deserted streets,
The muttering retreats
Of restless nights in one-night cheap hotels
And sawdust restaurants with oyster-shells:
Streets that follow like a tedious argument
Of insidious intent
To lead you to an overwhelming question …
Oh, do not ask, 'What is it?'
Let us go and make our visit.

In the room the women come and go
Talking of Michelangelo.

The yellow fog that rubs its back upon the window-panes,
The yellow smoke that rubs its muzzle on the window-panes,
Licked its tongue into the corners of the evening,
Lingered upon the pools that stand in drains,
Let fall upon its back the soot that falls from chimneys,
Slipped by the terrace, made a sudden leap,
And seeing that it was a soft October night,
Curled once about the house, and fell asleep.

266.

15th November, 1699. There happened this week so thick a mist and
fog, that people lost their way in the streets, it being so intense that
no light of candles, or torches, yielded any (or but very little)
direction. I was in it, and in danger. Robberies were committed

between the very lights which were fixed between London and
Kensington on both sides, and while coaches and travelers were
passing. It began about four in the afternoon, and was quite gone by
eight, without any wind to disperse it. At the Thames, they beat
drums to direct the watermen to make the shore.

267.

The evening oer the meadow seems to stoop
More distant lessens the diminished spire
Mist in the hollows reaks and curdles up
Like fallen clouds that spread – and things retire
Less seen and less – the shepherd passes near
And little distant most grotesquely shades
As walking without legs – lost to his knees
As through the rawky creeping smoke he wades
Now half way up the arches disappear
And small the bits of sky that glimmer through
Then trees loose all but tops – I meet the fields
And now the indistinctness passes bye
The shepherd all his length is seen again
And further on the village meets the eye

268.

Herein mists may well deserve the first place, as being, if not the first
in nature, yet the first meteor mentioned in Scripture, and soon after
the creation, for it is said, *Gen. ii.* that 'God had not yet caused it to
rain upon the earth, but a mist went up from the earth, and watered
the whole face of the ground,' for it might take a longer time for the
elevation of vapours sufficient to make a congregation of clouds able to
afford any store of showers and rain in so early days of the world (…)
    The great mist was not only observable about London, but in
remote parts of England, and as we hear, in Holland, so that it was of
larger extent than mists are commonly apprehended to be; most men
conceiving that they reach not much beyond the places where they
behold them. Mists make an obscure air, but they beget not darkness,

for the atoms and particles thereof admit the light, but if the matter thereof be very thick, close, and condensed, the mist grows considerably obscure and like a cloud, so the miraculous and palpable darkness of Egypt is conceived to have been effected by an extraordinary dense and dark mist or a kind of cloud spread over the land of Egypt, and also miraculously restrained from the neighbour land of Goshen.

There may be also subterraneous mists, when heat in the bowels of the earth, working upon humid parts, makes an attenuation thereof and consequently nebulous bodies in the cavities of it. There is a kind of a continued mist in the bodies of animals, especially in the cavous parts, as may be observed in bodies opened presently after death, and some think that in sleep there is a kind of mist in the brain; and upon exceeding motion some animals cast out a mist about them.

269.

> for now too nigh
Th' Archangel stood, and from the other hill
To their fixed station, all in bright array
The Cherubim descended; on the ground
Gliding meteorous, as Ev'ning Mist
Ris'n from a River o'er the marish glides,
And gathers ground fast at the Laborer's heel
Homeward returning.

270.

Ther was never so great a minde and spirit contayned in so little roome, so large an understandinge and so unrestrayned a fancy in so very small a body... and it may be the very remarkablenesse of his little person made the sharpnesse of his witt and the composed quicknesse of his judgement and understandinge, the more notable... Though every body loved his company very well, yett he loved very much to be alone, beinge in his constitution inclined somewhat to melancholique, and to retyrement amongst his bookes, and was so farr from being active, that he was contented to be reproched by his frendes with lazynesse, and was of so nice and tender a composition, that a little rayne or winde would disorder him, and diverte him from any shorte journy he had most willingly proposed to himselfe: insomuch as when he ridd abroade with those in whose company he most delighted, if the winde chanced to be in his face, he would (after a little pleasant murmuringe) suddaynely turne his horse, and goe home.

271.

Perhaps he found us perverse. He stayed away for more than twenty days; and then, I do not remember exactly when, I had a letter: 'Tell me clearly that you would like to see me and I shall come, though with some hesitation.'

I thought I would not answer, but my women argued that this would be cruel indeed, and finally I sent a single verse: 'Perhaps it would be best to follow whichever grass plumes beckon you.'

He replied by return messenger: 'When the grasses wave in the east wind, then surely I will follow.'

I sent back another poem: 'What good can the grasses do, putting out their plumes in the harsh autumn winds?'

So things went and presently he appeared, but we felt the usual constraint. He lay looking out at the garden – the flowers in the foreground were just then in full bloom – and wrote down a verse: 'Is it but the soft covering of dew that makes these colours flash so wildly?' And I answered: 'These flowers must face the autumn – you should know their wildness has that deeper source.'

It was towards the end of the month, and the late moon was just coming out when he showed signs of leaving. 'But perhaps I should stay?' he remarked tentatively, as though something in my manner indicated that I hoped he would. But I did not want him to think I was detaining him, and taking my brush I wrote a verse: 'If the moon takes upon itself to launch out into the sky, who am I to stop it?'

'Intent though it be on its passage through the sky, the moon leaves a shadow upon the waters,' he replied. 'If you want me to stay I shall stay.' And he did.

That autumn we had a violent storm, and two days later he called. 'Most people,' I remarked, 'would have sent to find out how I fared in the storm.' He may have seen the justice in my complaint, but he rolled off a poem with complete nonchalance: 'Better that I come as my own courier. The winds would have scattered my message.'

'It might have scattered your words, but still it was a friendly east wind, blowing my way.'

He pressed the argument with another verse: 'Am I to trust such a message to a foolish east wind? Think of the rumours it might have spread!'

'Very well. But why do you not ask, now that you have come?'

Once, in about the Tenth Month, an unusually violent rainstorm began just as he was getting ready to leave at night – on 'unavoidable' business.

'The winter rains will come, I know: but so late at night – and must you go?'

Paying no attention to my verse, he left. Has anyone ever been more outrageously insulted?

272.

As for *polysyllabical articulate Echoes*, the strongest and best I have met with here, is in the Park at Woodstock, which in the Day time, little wind being stirring, returns very *distinctly* Seventeen Syllables, and in the Night, Twenty: I made experiment of it with these Words,

> *Quae nec reticere loquenti*
> *Nec prior ipsa loqui didicit resonabilis Echo.*°

In the Day it would return only the last Verse, but in the Night, about Twelve a Clock, I could also hear the last Word of the former Hemistich (*loquenti*). The Object of which Echo, or the *Centrum phonocampticum*, I take to be the Hill with the Trees on the *summit* of it, about half a Mile distant from Woodstock Town, in the way thence to the Right Honourable the Earl of *Rochester's* Lodge: And the true place of the Speaker, or *Centrum phonicum*, the opposite Hill just without the Gate at the Towns-End, about Thirty Paces directly below the Corner of a Wall inclosing some Hay-ricks, near *Chaucer's* House . . .

That this Echo makes return of so many Syllables, and of a different number in the Day and Night, being indisputable and matter of fact; I proceed in the next place to the reasons of these certainties, which possibly to every body may not be so plain. First then, the causes why some Eccho's return more, and some fewer Syllables, I take to lye in the different distances of the objects (returning the Voice) from the place of the Speaker ...

The reason of the difference between Day and Night, why it should return seventeen Syllables in the one, and twenty in the other, may lie, I suppose, in the various qualities, and constitution of the *medium*, in different seasons; the Air being much more quiet, and stockt with exhalations in the Night than Day which something retarding the quick Motion of the Voice to the Object, and its return to the Speaker somewhat more, (by reason the Voice must needs be weakened in the Reflection) must necessarily give space for the return of more Syllables ...

° (*'resounding Echo, who could neither hold her peace when others spoke, nor yet begin to speak till others had addressed her.' – Ovid*)

273.

(*Approach of the storm*)

From the half
Of the sky
That which lives there
Is coming, and makes a noise.

274.

So Good luck came, and on my roofe did light,
Like noyse-less Snow, or as the dew of night:
Not all at once, but gently, as the trees
Are, by the Sun-beams, tickel'd by degrees.

275.

July 13, 1883. The comet – I have seen it at bedtime in the west, with head to the ground, white, a soft well-shaped tail, not big: I felt a certain awe and instress, a feeling of strangeness, of flight (it hangs like a shuttlecock at the height, before it falls) and of threatening.

276.

A comet blazed for seven nights together, rising always about eleven o'clock, visible to all in Rome. It was taken by all to be the soul of Caesar, now received into Heaven; for which reason, accordingly, Caesar is represented in his statue with a star on his brow.

277.

Nothing was more common, in those days, than to interpret all meteoric appearances, and other natural phenomena that occured with less regularity than the rise and set of sun and moon, as so many revelations from a supernatural source. Thus, a blazing spear, a sword of flame, a bow, or a sheaf of arrows seen in the midnight sky, prefigured Indian warfare. Pestilence was known to have been foreboded by a shower of crimson light. We doubt whether any marked event, for good or evil, ever befell New England, from its settlement down to revolutionary times, of which the inhabitants had not been previously warned by some spectacle of its nature. Not seldom, it had been seen by multitudes. Oftener, however, its credibility rested on the faith of some lonely eye-witness, who beheld the wonder through the coloured, magnifying, and distorted medium of his imagination, and shaped it more distinctly in his after-thought. It was, indeed, a majestic idea that the destiny of nations should be revealed, in these awful hieroglyphics, on the cope of heaven. A scroll so wide might not be deemed too expansive for Providence to write a people's doom upon. The belief was a favorite one with our forefathers, as betokening that their infant commonwealth was under a celestial guardianship of peculiar intimacy and strictness. But what shall we say, when an individual discovers a revelation addressed to himself alone, on the same vast sheet of record. In such a case, it could only be the symptom of a highly disordered mental state, when a man, rendered morbidly self-contemplative by long, intense, and secret pain, had extended his egotism over the whole expanse of nature, until the firmament itself should appear no more than a fitting page for his soul's history and fate.

278.

(written when the Duke of Modena ran away from the comet in the year 1742 or 1743)

> If at your coming princes disappear,
> Comets! Come every day – and stay a year.

279.

Now it is almost night, from the bronzey soft sky
jugfull after jugfull of pure white liquid fire, bright white
tipples over and spills down,
and is gone
and gold-bronze flutters bent through the thick upper air.

And as the electric liquid pours out, sometimes
a still brighter white snake wriggles among it, spilled
and tumbling wriggling down the sky:
and then the heavens cackle with uncouth sounds.

And the rain won't come, the rain refuses to come!

This is the electricity that man is supposed to have mastered
chained, subjugated to his use!
supposed to!

280.

Empedocles seems to think that sometimes we see because light leaves the eyes. At any rate, he says this: 'As when someone, intending a journey, prepares a lamp, a flame of flashing fire through the winter night, fastening the lantern-sides as protection against all the winds, which divert the breeze, but the light passes through to the outside, inasmuch as it is finer-textured, and illuminates the ground with its tireless rays: So then the ancient fire, imprisoned in the membranes and fine tissues, lies in ambush in the round pupil; and they hold back the deep water which flows around, but let the fire pass through inasmuch as it is finer-textured.' Sometimes he says we see in this way, sometimes by effluences from the objects seen.

281.

It was blacker than olives the night I left. As I ran past the palaces, oddly joyful, it began to rain. What a notion it is, after all – these small shapes! I would get lost counting them. Who first thought of it? How did he describe it to the others? Out on the sea it is raining too. It beats on no one.

282.

(*Enter BANQUO and FLEANCE with a torch*)

SECOND MURDERER.   A light, a light!
THIRD MURDERER.   'Tis he.
FIRST MURDERER.   Stand to't.
BANQUO. It will be rayne to-night.
FIRST MURDERER.   Let it come downe.
        (*They set upon BANQUO*)
BANQUO. O, Trecherie! Flye, good Fleance, flye, flye, flye!
                              (*Exit FLEANCE.*)

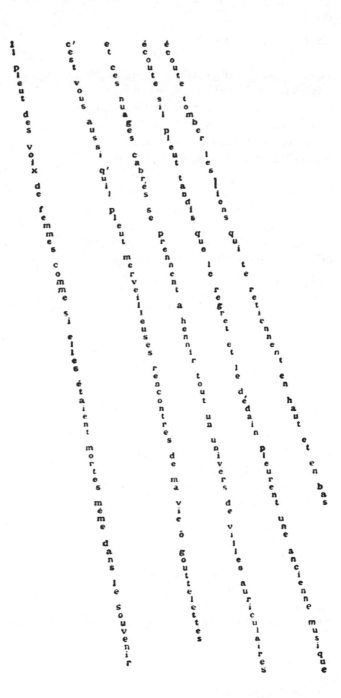

Il pleut des voix de femmes comme si elles étaient mortes même dans le souvenir

c'est vous aussi qu'il pleut merveilleuses rencontres de ma vie ô gouttelettes

et ces nuages cabrés se prennent a hennir tout un univers de villes auriculaires

écoute s'il pleut tandis que le regret et le dédain pleurent une ancienne musique

écoute tomber les liens qui te retiennent en haut et en bas

284.

(The heath. Before a hovel.)

KING LEAR. Prythee go in thy selfe, seeke thine owne ease,
This tempest will not give me leave to ponder
On things would hurt me more, but I'le goe in,
In Boy, go first. You houselesse povertie,
Nay get thee in; I'le pray, and then I'le sleepe.
Poor naked wretches, where so e're you are
That bide the pelting of this pittilesse storme,
How shall your houselesse heads, and unfed sides,
Your loop'd and window'd raggednesse defend you
From seasons such as these? O, I have ta'en
Too little care of this! Take Physicke, Pomp;
Expose thy selfe to feele what wretches feele,
That thou mayst shake the superflux to them,
And shew the Heavens more just.

285.

When I'm lying awake, listening to rain
hammering on the roof,
the phrase comes back to me,
our code for 'Let's get out of here'.
We were huddled in the back of a van
with the lights, the videotape equipment
and the man with the rain machine.
'Why can't we use the regular rain?' you asked,
as rain hammered on the roof.
'That's God's rain', said someone.
'It doesn't show up on film.
We need Billy's rain for this one.'
When I find myself soaked to the skin, tired,
or merely bored with God's rain,
the phrase comes back to me.
I'd say it now if I thought you were listening.

286.

The weather is overtaking us with its March squalls. They scurry across the rainy sky, scarcely allowing it the time for a downpour; and suddenly everything lies naked, and an unwonted lucency, almost vacant, shines up from the damp streets. It has been like that all night. Do you know that when I am in the city I am actually frightened by such nocturnal hurricanes. It is as though, in their elemental pride, they did not see us. But they do see a lonely house in the country; they take it in their rugged arms and, in this way they inure it, and when you are there, you would like to be out-of-doors, in the roaring garden, or at least, stand at the window and applaud the infuriated old trees that twist and turn as though possessed by the spirits of the prophets.

287.

> 'Of these the vigilance
> I dread, and to elude, thus wrapt in mist
> Of midnight vapor glide obscure, and prie
> In every Bush and Brake, where hap may finde
> The Serpent sleeping, in whose mazie foulds
> To hide me, and the dark intent I bring' (...)
> So saying, through each Thicket Danck or Drie,
> Like a black mist low creeping, he held on
> His midnight search, where soonest he might finde
> The Serpent: him fast sleeping soon he found
> In Labyrinth of many a round self-rowld,
> His head the midst, well stor'd with suttle wiles

288.

(*Enter the King of Fairies at one doore with his train, and the Queen at another with hers*)

TITANIA. And never, since the middle Summers spring,
Met we on hil, in dale, forrest or mead,
By pavèd fountain or by rushie brooke,

Or in the beachèd margent of the sea,
To dance our ringlets to the whistling Winde,
But with thy brawls thou hast disturb'd our sport.
Therefore the Windes, piping to us in vaine,
As in revenge, have suck'd up from the sea
Contagious fogges; which falling in the Land,
Have everie pelting River made so proud
That they have over-borne their Continents:
The Oxe hath therefore stretch'd his yoake in vaine,
The Ploughman lost his sweat, and the greene Corne
Hath rotted, ere his youth attain'd a beard:
The fold stands empty in the drownèd field,
And Crowes are fatted with the murrion flocke;
The nine men's Morris is fill'd up with mud,
And the quaint Mazes in the wanton green
For lack of tread are undistinguishable.
The humane mortals want their winter heere;
No night is now with hymne or caroll blest:
Therefore the Moone (the governesse of floods)
Pale in her anger, washes all the aire,
That Rheumaticke diseases doe abound:
And thorough this distemperature, we see
The seasons alter: hoary-headed frosts
Fall in the fresh lap of the crimson Rose,
And on old *Hiems'* thin and icie crowne
An odorous Chaplet of sweet Sommer buds
Is, as in mockery, set. The Spring, the Sommer,
The childing Autumne, angry Winter, change
Their wonted Liveries, and the mazèd world,
By their increase, now knowes not which is which:
And this same progeny of evills comes
From our debate, from our dissention;
We are their parents and originall.
OBERON. Do you amend it then; it lies in you:
Why should *Titania* cross her *Oberon*?

289.

Precisely at twelve o'clock a strange rectangular block of fire appeared
in the east-south-east. Its size was that of a small tabular iceberg, but
it had a dull crimson glow which made the scene at once weird and
fascinating. Its base rested on the horizon and it seemed to rise,
brighten, and move northerly. The sky here was purple, thinly veiled
by a light smoky haze, caused by icy crystals in the lower stratus of
atmosphere, but there was not another speck of redness on this side
of the heavens except the orange bow usually seen over the twilight
zone. We watched this with considerable awe and amazement for ten
minutes before we could determine its meaning. It passed through
several stages of forms, finally it separated, and we discovered that it
was the moon.

290.

Monday April 12, 1802 – Walked to T. Wilkinson's and sent for letters.
The woman brought me one from Wm and Mary. It was a sharp
windy night. Thomas Wilkinson came with me to Barton, and
questioned me like a catechizer all the way. Every question was like
the snapping of a little thread about my heart I was so full of thoughts
of my half-read letter and other things. I was glad when he left me.
Then I had time to look at the moon while I was thinking over my
own thoughts. The moon travelled through the clouds tingeing them
yellow as she passed along, with two stars near her, one larger than
the other. These stars grew or diminished as they passed from or went
into the clouds. At this time William as I found the next day was
riding by himself between Middleham and Barnard Castle having
parted from Mary. I read over my letter when I got to the house.
Mr. and Mrs. C[oleridge] were playing at cards.

291.

A Tartar horn tugs at the north wind,
Thistle Gate shines whiter than the stream.
The sky swallows the road to Kokonor.
On the Great Wall, a thousand miles of moonlight.

The dew comes down, the banners drizzle,
Cold bronze rings the watches of the night.
The nomads' armour meshes serpents' scales.
Horses neigh, Evergreen Mound is champed white.

In the still of autumn see the Pleiades.
Far out on the sands, danger in the furze.
North of their tents is surely the sky's end
Where the sound of the river streams beyond the border.

292.

20 September 1814. The ear-deceiving Imitation of a steady soaking
Rain, while the Sky is in full uncurtainment of sprinkled Stars and
milky Stream and dark blue Interspaces – the Rain had held up for
two Hours or more – but so deep was the silence of the Night, that
the *Drip* from the Leaves of the Garden Trees *copied* a steady Shower –

293.

In the uncertain hour before the morning
        Near the ending of interminable night
        At the recurrent end of the unending
After the dark dove with the flickering tongue
        Had passed below the horizon of his homing
        While the dead leaves still rattled on like tin
Over the asphalt where no other sound was
        Between three districts whence the smoke arose
        I met one walking, loitering and hurried
As if blown towards me like the metal leaves
        Before the urban dawn wind unresisting.
        And as I fixed upon the down-turned face
That pointed scrutiny with which we challenge
        The first-met stranger in the waning dusk
        I caught the sudden look of some dead master
Whom I had known, forgotten, half recalled
        Both one and many; in the brown baked features

The eyes of a familiar compound ghost
Both intimate and unidentifiable.
So I assumed a double part, and cried
And heard another's voice cry: 'What! are *you* here?'
Although we were not. I was still the same,
Knowing myself yet being someone other –
And he a face still forming; yet the words sufficed
To compel the recognition they preceded.
And so, compliant to the common wind,
Too strange to each other for misunderstanding,
In concord at this intersection time
Of meeting nowhere, no before and after,
We trod the pavement in a dead patrol.

294.

After going to sleep, his imagination was struck by the appearance of some phantoms who appeared to him and who frightened him so much that, thinking he was walking through the streets, he was forced to turn over on his left side in order to get to the place where he wanted to go, because he felt a great weakness on his right side, on which he could not support himself. Ashamed of proceeding in this fashion, he made an effort to stand up, but he felt a wind-storm which, carrying him along in a sort of whirlwind, made him make three or four pirouettes on his left foot.

So far this did not frighten him. The difficulty he had in dragging himself along made him expect to fall at each step, until he saw along his route an open college and went into it to find shelter and a remedy for his problem. He tried to reach the chapel, where he first thought he would go to pray, but realizing that he had passed a man of his acquaintance without greeting him, he wished to retrace his steps to address him properly and was violently hurled back by the wind which drove him back towards the chapel. At the same time he saw in the middle of the college courtyard someone else, who in a respectful and polite fashion called him by name and said to him that if he was willing to go find Monsieur N., he had something to give him. M. Descartes fancied that it was a melon which had been imported from some foreign country. But what surprised him more was to see that the people who joined this man in gathering around to converse with him were erect and steady on their feet, while he, standing in the same place, remained bent and staggering, and that the wind, which he had thought several times would blow him over, had greatly diminished. With this fancy in mind he woke up, with twinges of sharp pain in his left side. He did not know whether he was dreaming or awake. Half-awake, he told himself that an evil genius was trying to seduce him, and he murmured a prayer to exorcise it.

He went to sleep again. A clap of thunder woke him again and filled his room with flashes. Once more he asked himself whether he was asleep or awake, whether it was a dream or a day-dream, opening and shutting his eyes so as to reach a certainty. Then, reassured, he dozed off, swept away by exhaustion.

295.

Benedicite! what dremyd I this nyght?
Methought the worlde was turnyd upsodowne
the son the moone hade lost ther force and lyght
the see also drownyd both towre and towne.
Yett more mervell how that I hard the sownde
of onys voice saying: bere in thy mynd
thy lady hath forgoten to be kynd.

296.

    The fifth year of the new Son of Heaven,
    The cyclic year Keng-yin;
    The season when the handle of the Dipper sticks into Aries,
    The month when the pitch-tune is Yellow Bell.
Ten thousand forest trees stood rigid in the night:
The cold air tensed against us, solid and windless.
The glittering silver dish rose from the bottom of the sea,
Came forth and lighted the East of my thatched cottage.
On heaven's smooth and violet surface the freezing light stopped flowing,
Rays from the ice pierced and crossed the cold glimmer of moonrise.
    At first it seemed that a white lotus
    Had floated up from the Dragon King's palace.

But this night, the fifteenth of the eighth month,
Was not like other nights;
For now we saw a strange thing:
There was something easing its way inside the rim.
The rim was as though a strong man hacked off pieces with an axe,
The cassia was like a snowy peak dragged and tumbled by the wind.
The mirror refined a hundredfold
Till it shone right through to the gall
Suddenly was buried in cold ash:
The pearl of the fiery dragon
Which flew up out of its brain
Went back into the oyster's womb.
Ring and disc crumbled away as I watched,
Darkness smeared the whole sky like soot,
Rubbing out in an instant the last tracks,
And then it seemed like for thousands of ages the sky would never open.
Who would guess that a thing so magical
Could be so discomfited?
The stars came out like sprinkled sand
Disputing which could shine the brightest,
And the lamps lit by the servants
With a dusky glow like tortoiseshell
This night spat flames like long rainbows
Shooting from the houses through holes and cracks
into a thousand roads (…)
I know how the school of Yin and Yang explains it:
'When the sun devours the moon, moonlight is quenched,
When the moon covers the sun, sunlight fails.'
But the two eyes do not attack each other;
This theory does not convince me.
Better what Lao-tzu said, who taught Confucius:
'The five colours blind men's eyes.'
I fear that Heaven, just like man,
Can lose its sight by lusting after beauty.
But the time is wrong, it is not Spring,
All things have passed their prime of loveliness,
The blue of the hills is the colour of broken shards,
The ice piles mountain-high on the green water,

The flowers have withered, their woman's charm all gone,
The birds are dead, their songs vanished.
In brutish winter what is there to love
For Heaven to gaze on till an eye goes blind?

297.

A dream once occurred to me wherein the mythical character almost
assumed the dimensions of the sublime, insomuch that I can scarcely
recall it without awe. I dreamed that I was standing on a certain broad
grassy space in the park of my old home. It was totally dark, but I was
aware that I was in the midst of an immense crowd. We were all gazing
upward into the murky sky, and a sense of some fearful calamity was
over us, so that no one spoke aloud. Suddenly overhead appeared,
through a rift in the black heavens, a branch of stars which I
recognized as the belt and sword of Orion. Then went forth a cry of
despair from all our hearts! We knew, though no one said it, that these
stars proved it was not a cloud or mist, which, as we had somehow
believed, was causing the darkness. No; the air was clear; it was high
noon, and the sun had not risen! That was the tremendous reason why
we beheld the stars. The sun would never rise again! In this dream, as it
seems to me, a very complicated myth was created by my unconscious
brain, which having first by some chance stumbled on the picture of a
crowd in the dark, and a bit of starry sky over them, elaborated, to
account for such facts, the bold theory of the sun not having risen at
noon; or (if we like to take it the other way) having hit on the idea of
the sun's disappearance, invented the appropriate scenery of the
breathless expectant crowd, and the apparition of the stars.

298.

The first man holds it in his hands
He holds the sun in his hands
In the centre of the sky, he holds it in his hands
As he holds it in his hands, it starts upward.

The first woman holds it in her hands
She holds the moon in her hands

In the centre of the sky, she holds it in her hands
As she holds it in her hands, it starts upward.

The first man holds it in his hands
He holds the sun in his hands
In the centre of the sky, he holds it in his hands
As he holds it in his hands, it starts downward.

The first woman holds it in her hands
She holds the moon in her hands
In the centre of the sky, she holds it in her hands
As she holds it in her hands, it starts downward.

299.

Are you asleep my friend? Rise and awake the dawn, look up to
heaven. See, it is like a leopard's skin, all covered with spots. And see
how the half moon – which should be full on this night – is as black
as the mouth of an oven or the rim of a pot; like the face of a girl, half
flushed and half in shadow.

Now look again, at this month's end, and see the sun, almost engulfed
by gloom. What little light remains upon its darkness is like a diadem
on the head of a negress. And the earth, as if in mourning for its sun,
is like a woman disfigured by tears.

He who is master of might and beauty, He struck both his luminaries
in the very same month. He covered the face of the moon with His
terrestrial globe and blocked off the sun with His moon. All this was
done by God, who does as He wishes with His works.

From the very beginning He put some shadow in the moon, but the
sun He created pure. Therefore – as they now dim, in this darkness
that has come to pass – I compare them to two women: the one with
bruises on her face, the other with bruises and sores.

He darkened the light of day in mid-morning, and the light of night
at midnight, like a raging king who harasses all his Lords in their

own domains. First He struck the nightlight, and only later did He strike the light of day, like a king who gives a stupefying drink first to his maidservant and afterwards to his queen.

300.

Thursday, June 30th.

Now I must sketch out the Eclipse.

About 10 on Tuesday night several very long trains, accurately filled (ours with civil servants) left Kings Cross. In our carriage were Vita, Harold, Quentin, L. and I. This is Hatfield I daresay, I said. I was smoking a cigar. Then again, This is Peterborough, L. said. Before it got dark we kept looking at the sky; soft fleecy; but there was one star, over Alexandra Park. Look, Vita, that's Alexandra Park, said Harold. The Nicolsons got sleepy; H. curled up with his head on V.'s knee. She looked like Sappho by Leighton, asleep; so we plunged through the midlands; made a very long stay at York. Then at 3 we got out our sandwiches and I came in from the WC to find Harold being rubbed clean of cream. Then he broke the china sandwich box. Here L. laughed without restraint. Then we had another doze, or the N.'s did; then here was a level crossing, at which were drawn up a long line of motor omnibuses and motors, all burning pale yellow lights. It was getting grey – still a fleecy mottled sky. We got to Richmond about 3.30; it was cold, and the N.'s had a quarrel, Eddie said, about V.'s luggage. We went off in the omnibus (…)

There were also many motor cars. These suddenly increased as we crept up to the top of Bardon Fell. Here were people camping beside their cars. We got out and found ourselves very high, on a moor, boggy, heathery, with butts for grouse shooting. There were grass tracks here and there and people had already taken up positions. So we joined them, walking out to what seemed the highest point looking over Richmond. One light burned down there. Vales and moors stretched, slope after slope, round us. It was like the Haworth country. But over Richmond, where the sun was rising, was a soft grey cloud. We could see by a gold spot where the sun was. But it was early yet. We had to wait, stamping to keep warm, (…) Leonard kept looking at his watch. Four great red setters came leaping over the moor. There were sheep feeding behind us. (…) There were thin places in the clouds and some complete holes. The question was whether the sun would show through a cloud or through one of these hollow places when the time came. We began to get anxious. We saw rays coming through the bottom of the clouds. Then, for a moment, we saw the sun sweeping – it seemed to be sailing at a great pace and clear in a gap; we had out our smoked glasses; we saw it Crescent, burning red; next moment it had sailed fast into the cloud again; only the red streamers came from it; then only a golden haze, such as one has often seen. The moments were passing. We thought we were cheated; we looked at the sheep; they showed no fear; the setters were racing round; everyone was standing in long lines, rather dignified, looking out. I thought how we were like very old people, in the birth of the world – druids on Stonehenge (this idea came more vividly in the first pale light though). At the back of us were great blue spaces in the cloud. These were still blue. But now the colour was going out. The clouds were turning pale; a reddish black colour. Down in the valley it was an extraordinary scrumble of red and black; there was the one light burning; all was cloud down there, and very beautiful, so delicately tinted. Nothing could be seen through the cloud. The 24 seconds were passing. Then one looked back again at the blue: and rapidly, very very quickly, all the colours faded; it became darker and darker as at the beginning of a violent storm; the light sank and sank; we kept saying this is the shadow; and we thought now it is over – this is the shadow; when suddenly the light went out. We had fallen. It was extinct. There was no colour. The earth was dead. That was the astonishing moment; and the next when as if a ball had rebounded the cloud took colour on itself again, only a sparky ethereal colour and so the light came back. I had very strongly the feeling as the light went out of some vast obeisance; something kneeling down and suddenly raised up when the colours came. The colour for some moments was of the most lovely kind – fresh, various; here blue and there brown; all new colours, as if washed over and repainted. They came back astonishingly lightly and quickly and beautifully in the valley and over the hills – at first with a miraculous glittering and etheriality, later normally almost, but with a great sense of relief. It was like recovery. We had been much worse than we had expected. We had seen the world dead. This was within the power of nature. Our greatness had been apparent too. Now we became Ray in a blanket, Saxon in a cap etc. We were bitterly cold. I should say that the cold had increased as the light went down. One felt very livid. Then – it was over till 1999.

ACKNOWLEDGEMENTS

'Right On'. Copyright © 1972 by A.R. Ammons, from THE COMPLETE POEMS OF A.R. AMMONS: VOLUME 1 1955–1977 by A.R. Ammons, edited by Robert M. West. Used by permission of W. W. Norton & Company, Inc.

'Il Pleut' by Guillaume Apollinaire, translated by Roger Shattuck, from SELECTED WRITINGS, copyright © 1971 by Roger Shattuck. Reprinted by permission of New Directions Publishing Corp.

The use of 117 (one hundred and seventeen) words from THE BIRDS AND OTHER PLAYS written by Aristophanes and translated with introductory matter by David Barrett and Alan H. Sommerstein (Penguin Classics, 2003). This translation first published 1978. Reprinted with a Select Bibliography 2003. Copyright © David Barrett and Alan H. Sommerstein, 1978. Reproduced by permission of Penguin Books Ltd.

The use of 252 (two hundred and fifty-two) words from LYSISTRATA AND OTHER PLAYS written by Aristophanes and translated by Alan H. Sommerstein (Penguin Classics, 2003). Original translation first published 1973. This revised edition first published 2002. Copyright © Alan H. Sommerstein, 2002. Reproduced by permission of Penguin Books Ltd.

Excerpt from "The Words Of The All-Wise." Copyright © 1969 by W.H. Auden, renewed. Reprinted by permission of Curtis Brown, Ltd. Excerpt from "Norse Riddle." Copyright © 1981 by W.H. Auden, renewed. Reprinted by permission of Curtis Brown, Ltd. Excerpt from "The Song Of The Sun." Copyright © 1981 by W.H. Auden, renewed. Reprinted by permission of Curtis Brown, Ltd.

The use of 126 (one hundred and twenty-six) words from *Early Greek Philosophy* by Jonathan Barnes (Penguin Classics, 2004). First published

'A Breezy Day' reprinted by courtesy of the Estate of Ian Hamilton Finlay.

'Anatomy of Winter (After Hesiod)' by Robert Garioch, from *Robert Garioch: Collected Poems* (2004). Published by Birlinn, Ltd. Reproduced with permission of the Licensor through PLSclear.

'Enter a Cloud' from *New Collected Poems* by W. S. Graham. Copyright © 2005 by the Estate of W. S. Graham. Reproduced by permission of Faber and Faber and the Estate of W. S. Graham.

'The Wind' (trans. Gwyneth Lewis) by Dafydd ap Gwilym. Reproduced by permission of Antony Harwood Ltd.

Quote from p. 99 from *Basic Writings* by Martin Heidegger. English translation © 1977, 1993 by HarperCollins Publishers Inc. Used by permission of HarperCollins Publishers.

Excerpt from HIROSHIMA by John Hersey, copyright © 1946, 1985, copyright renewed 1973 by John Hersey. Used by permission of Alfred A. Knopf, an imprint of the Knopf Doubleday Publishing Group, a division of Penguin Random House LLC. All rights reserved.

The use of 109 (one hundred and nine) words from *Essays and Letters* written by Friedrich Hölderlin and translated and edited by Jeremy Adler and Charlie Louth (Penguin Classics, 2009). This edition first published in Penguin Classics, 2009. Selection, translation and editorial material copyright © Jeremy Adler and Charlie Louth, 2009. Reproduced by permission of Penguin Books Ltd.

'Brief reflections on maps' (trans. Ewald Osers) by Miroslav Holub, from *Poems Before & After: Collected English Translations* (trans. Ian and Jarmila Milner et al.). Reproduced with permission of Bloodaxe Books.

'Wind' from COLLECTED POEMS by Ted Hughes. Copyright © 2003 by The Estate of Ted Hughes. Reprinted by permission of Farrar, Straus, and Giroux and Faber and Faber Ltd.

'Notes on Blindness' by John M. Hull. © John M. Hull. Reprinted by permission of Wellcome Collection and the author.

Excerpt from *The Camera and I* by Joris Ivens. © Joris Ivens 1969. Reprinted by permission of International Publishers.

In Parenthesis by David Jones. Reprinted by permission of Faber and Faber Ltd.

Extract from *Sounds (Klänge)* by Vassily Kandinsky (trans. Tony Frazer). Bristol: Shearsman Books, 2018. Translation copyright © Tony Frazer 2018.

Excerpt from *The Emperor* by Ryszard Kapuscinski. Copyright © 1983 by Ryszard Kapuscinski. Used by permission of Houghton Mifflin Harcourt. All rights reserved.

Excerpt from *Essays on Idleness* by Yoshida Kenko. Translation © 1998 by Donald Keene. Reprinted with permission of Columbia University Press.

Extract from *The Six-Cornered Snowflake* by Johannes Kepler (trans. C. Hardie). Published by Oxford University Press. Reproduced with permission of the Licensor through PLSclear.

'Skybooks' by Velimir Khlebnikov, from THE COLLECTED WORKS OF VELIMIR KHLEBNIKOV: VOLUME I – LETTERS AND THEORETICAL WRITINGS, translated by Paul Schmidt, edited by Charlotte Douglas, Cambridge, Mass.: Harvard University Press, Copyright © 1987 by the Dia Art Foundation.

'Absences' from THE COMPLETE POEMS OF PHILIP LARKIN by Philip Larkin, edited by Archie Burnet. Copyright © 2012 by The Estate of Philip Larkin. Reprinted by permission of Farrar, Straus, and Giroux, and Faber and Faber Ltd.

Excerpts from 'Trees in the Garden' and 'Storm in the Black Forest' from THE CAMBRIDGE EDITION OF THE WORKS OF DH LAWRENCE: THE POEMS by DH Lawrence. © Cambridge University Press 2013. Reproduced by permission of Paper Lion Ltd, The Estate of Frieda Lawrence Ravagli and Cambridge University Press.

'On the Frontier' by Li Ho and 'The Eclipse of the Moon' by Lu T'ung (trans. A. C. Graham), from *Poems of the Late T'Ang*. Published in

English by New York Review Books. Translation copyright © 1965, 1977 by A. C. Graham.

Excerpts from 'Struck by Lightning' and 'Explicit Snow' from *The Poems of Norman MacCaig* (2010) by Norman MacCaig. Copyright © Norman MacCaig. Published by Birlinn, Ltd. Reproduced with permission of the Licensor through PLSclear.

'Snow' by Louis MacNeice, from *Collected Poems*. Published by Faber & Faber and reproduced by permission of David Higham Associates Limited.

'The Snow Party' by Derek Mahon, from *New Selected Poems*. Copyright © Derek Mahon 2016. '(On Clouds)' by Lucretius, translation © Derek Mahon 2005. Reproduced by kind permission of the author and the Gallery Press, Loughcrew, Oldcastle, County Meath, Ireland.

Excerpt from *Rejuvenating Medical Education* by Robert Marshall and Alan Bleakley. Reproduced by permission of Cambridge Scholars Publishing.

'The Boundary Commission' and 'Why Brownlee Left' from POEMS 1968–1998 by Paul Muldoon. Reprinted by permission of Farrar, Straus, and Giroux, and Faber and Faber Ltd.

'Two Rains' by Les Murray, from *Dog Fox Field*. Copyright © 1993 by Les A Murray. Reproduced by permission of the Margaret Connolly Agency and Farrar, Straus, and Giroux.

'A True Account of Talking to the Sun at Fire Island,' and 'Joe's Jacket' from THE COLLECTED POEMS OF FRANK O'HARA by Frank O'Hara, copyright © 1971 by Maureen Granville-Smith, Administratrix of the Estate of Frank O'Hara, copyright renewed 1999 by Maureen O'Hara Granville-Smith and Donald Allen. Used by permission of Alfred A. Knopf, an imprint of the Knopf Doubleday Publishing Group, a division of Penguin Random House LLC. All rights reserved.

'The knowledge not of sorrow' by George Oppen, from *New Collected Poems*. Copyright © 1932 by George Oppen. Reprinted by permission of New Directions Publishing Corp.

The Poems of Exile: Tristia and the Black Sea Letters, by Ovid and translated by Peter Green, © 2005 by the Regents of the University of California. Reprinted by permission of the University of California Press.

Extract from *Songs of Gods, Songs of Humans: The Epic Tradition of the Ainu* by Donald L. Phillip. Copyright © 1979 by University of Tokyo Press. Published and reprinted by permission of Princeton University Press.

'Rain' by Francis Ponge, translated by Peter Riley, from *The Random House Book of Twentieth Century French Poetry* (New York: Random House, 1984), used with the kind permission of Peter Riley.

'Martial, *Epigrams*, IV.18' by Peter Porter, from *The Rest on the Flight: Selected Poems* (2010). © Peter Porter. Published by Picador, a division of Pan MacMillan. Reproduced with permission of the Licensor through PLSclear.

'In a Station of the Metro', 'Lament of the Frontier Guard', 'The Jewel Stairs' Grievance' and 'The Seafarer' by Ezra Pound, from *Personae*. Copyright © 1926 by Ezra Pound. Reprinted by permission of New Directions Publishing Corp.

'Dandelions' by Craig Raine, from *Collected Poems 1978–1998*. Published by Picador & Faber and reproduced by permission of David Higham Associates Limited.

'First Rain' by Yannis Ritsos, translated by Rae Dalven. Translation © 1977 by Rae Dalven. Reprinted by permission of the A. S. Onassis Program in Hellenic Studies at New York University and the estate of Yannis Ritsos.

'July 11, 1968, Rain', from SOBBING SUPERPOWER: SELECTED POEMS OF TADEUSZ RÓŻEWICZ by Tadeusz Różewicz, translated by Joanna Trzeciak. Copyright © 2011 by Joanna Trzeciak. Used by permission of W. W. Norton & Company, Inc.

Excerpt from *Memoirs of My Nervous Illness* by Daniel Paul Schreber. Published in English by New York Review Books. Copyright © 1955 by the President and Fellows of Harvard College. Reprinted by permission.

'The Dwarf Pine' by Varlam Shalamov, from *Kolyma Tales* (1960). Published in English by New York Review Books. Copyright © 2018 by Alexander Rigosik. Translation copyright © 2018 by Donald Rayfield. Reprinted with permission.

Extract from *The Living Mountain: A Celebration of the Cairngorm Mountains of Scotland* by Nan Shepherd. Copyright © Nan Shepherd, 1977. Reproduced by permission of Canongate Books Ltd.

'At the Bomb Testing Site' by William Stafford, from *Ask Me: 100 Essential Poems*. Copyright © 1960, 2014 by William Stafford and the Estate of William Stafford. Reprinted with the permission of The Permissions Company, LLC on behalf of Graywolf Press, Minneapolis, Minnesota, www.graywolfpress.org

'A Clear Day and No Memories' and 'The Snow Man' by Wallace Stevens, from *The Collected Poems of Wallace Stevens*. Copyright © 1954 by Wallace Stevens and copyright renewed 1982 by Holly Stevens. Used by permission of Faber and Faber Ltd. and Alfred A. Knopf, an imprint of the Knopf Doubleday Publishing Group, a division of Penguin Random House LLC. All rights reserved.

'Utah' by Anne Stevenson, from *Poems 1955–2005*. Reproduced with permission of Bloodaxe Books.

Extract from *My Cocaine Museum* by Michael Taussig. Reprinted by permission of the University of Chicago Press.

'Fragment' by Stephen Watts, © Stephen Watts 1979. Reprinted by permission of the author.

'Billy's Rain' by Hugo Williams, from *Collected Poems*. Reprinted by permission of Faber and Faber Ltd.

All unattributed translations are by the editors.

GLOSSARY

Robert Garioch, 'The Anatomy of Winter'

felloun cruel; *flype* flay, turn inside out; *nowt* ox; *brulyies* embroil; *gars* causes to; *blawp* heave up water; *warsle* wrestle; *dunt* thud; *gowls* hollows; *girns* cries; *garrs the bestiall grue* makes the beasts shiver; *hurdies* buttocks; *yins* ones; *cleidin* covering; *weill-happit* well-protected; *gait* goat; *gimmers* two-year old sheep; *fouth* plenty; *flegs* frightens; *skaith* harm; *bienlie* in a state of well-being; *ongauns* goings-on; *ben the hous* in the innermost room; *baneless yin* boneless one (the octopus) *tholan* enduring; *dowie* dismal; *sairs* serves; *swees* swings; *sweirt* unwilling; *hirsel* herd; *thirlit in aefald thocht* joined by a single thought; *bield* shelter; *boss* hollow; *Trauchlit in siccan times* hard-pressed in such times; *luttaird loons* bowed wretches; *lunyie* loins; *hirple* limp; *hap-schackellit* hobbled; *hainan* saving; *puckle* little; *birssy* bristling; *lappits* flaps; *neb* nose; *nithert* chilled; *hairst* harvest; *bieldan* protecting; *haar* mist; *deray* disturbance; *ruggan* tugging fiercely; *thwankan cluddis* clouds mingling in thick and gloomy procession; *thruschit* thrust

Hugh MacDiarmid, 'The Sauchs in the Reuch Heuch Hauch'

teuch tough; *sauchs* willow-trees; *Reuch Heuch Hauch* the name of a field near Hawick in the Scottish Borders; *ilk ane* each one; *birlin'* whirling round; *hert* heart; *thrawn* contrary, twisted; *a hanlawhile* a little while; *amplefeyst* contrariness

Sir Gawain and the Green Knight

renk knight; *Logres* (Arthur's kingdom); *thagh* though; *leudles* without company; *lenges* remains; *fare* entertainment; *fere* companion; *fole* horse; *frythes* woods; *gome* man; *bi gate* on the road; *to karp* to speak of; *neghed* approached; *forlondes* headlands; *Holy-Hede* Holyhead; *eft* again; *bonk* reached the shore; *Wyrale* Wirral; *11-12* few lived there whom either God or good-hearted men loved (. . .) *floten* travelled; *fremedly* as a stranger; *uche* each; *warthe* ford; *other* or; *wye* knight; *bot ferly hit were* or else it was a wonder; *felle* fierce; *to tore* too difficult; *dole* part; *sumwhyle* sometimes; *wormes* dragons; *als* also; *wodwos* trolls; *woned* lived; *knarres* crags; *etaynes* giants, ogres; *anelede* pursued; *doghty* doughty; *drye* resolute; *Dryghtyn* the Lord God; *dreped* killed; *werre* fighting; *wrathed* afflicted; *fres* froze; *fale* pale; *slete* sleet; *yrnes* armour; *innoghe* enough; *borne* burn, stream

William Dunbar, 'In to thir dirk and drublie dayis'

In to thir in these; *drublie* cloudy; *Quhone* when; *sabil* black; *curage . . . of* appetite for; *ballatis* ballads; *8* my dismal spirit cowers under threat; *dois forloir* is forlorn; *mair* more; *remeid* remedy; *assayit* assailed; *leif* live; *mischeif* hardship; *abyd* dwell; *wirk furthe* work off; *glas* hourglass; *hald that will away* keep what will pass; *28* or crave what you cannot keep; *tending* moving; *32* and do not act like a stranger, I request you; *compt* account; *36* then Death throws his gates wide open; *albeid* although; *stout* strong; *lintal* lintel; *lowt* stoop; *drowp* am dejected; *kist* chest; *cowp* goblet; *lat* prevent; *sowp* sup; *disport* pleasure

INDEX OF AUTHORS AND TITLES